THE PURPOSE OF PLANNING

Creating sustainable towns and cities

Yvonne Rydin

First published in Great Britain in 2011 by

Policy Press
University of Bristol
1-9 Old Park Hill
Bristol
BS2 8BB
UK
t: +44 (0)117 954 5940
pp-info@bristol.ac.uk
www.policypress.co.uk

North America office:
Policy Press
c/o The University of Chicago Press
1427 East 60th Street
Chicago, IL 60637, USA
t: +1 773 702 7700
f: +1 773-702-9756
sales@press.uchicago.edu
www.press.uchicago.edu

British Library Cataloguing in Publication Data
A catalogue record for this book is available from the British Library

Library of Congress Cataloging-in-Publication Data
A catalog record for this book has been requested

ISBN 978 1 84742 430 3 paperback

Cover design by Policy Press
Front cover: photograph kindly supplied by Getty
Printed and bound in Great Britain by CMP, Poole

Contents

—

Preface

My aim in writing this book was to provide an accessible introduction to the planning system, particularly as it operates in the UK, but with the emphasis on the questions and issues that make people interested in planning. I wanted to connect with the reasons why planning is such an intriguing area to study and why it raises such strong feelings when people engage with it. As I finalised the text, the new Conservative-led coalition government made its first policy announcements and the press was full of coverage about 'garden-grabbing' and giving planning powers back to local government. Radio phone-ins are never short of callers when planning is being debated and local newspapers rely on planning topics to fill their papers and give them their banner headlines.

It is clear that planning matters. It is impossible to walk down a street at home or visit a new locality on holiday (if the family is unfortunate enough to contain a planner) without seeing something that is the object of planning activity or should be. Academically the study of planning is usually confined to geography (where it has a strong presence throughout secondary school and even before that) and to planning schools. But planning matters to everyone because we all live within built and natural environments that are planned.

I hope this little book provides an insight into exactly why and how it matters. It is not a heavy academic treatise; I have deliberately kept the referencing light and abandoned the Harvard system with its annoying interruptions of the text. Thanks to The Policy Press for being so accommodating on this and to the Bartlett School of Planning for indulging my desire to write this book.

Yvonne Rydin
London, 24 June 2010

ONE

Why plan?

Six magnificent boulevards – each 120 feet wide –
traverse the city from centre to circumference, dividing
it into six equal parts or wards. In the centre is a circular
space containing about five and a half acres, laid out as
a beautiful and well-watered garden; and, surrounding
this garden, each standing in its own ample grounds, are
the larger public buildings – town hall, principal concert
and lecture hall, theatre, library, museum, picture-gallery,
and hospital. The rest of the large space encircled by the
'Crystal Palace' is a public park, containing 145 acres,
which includes ample recreation grounds within very
easy access of all the people.[1]

Every utopia contains an imagined home or city or landscape;
this one comes from Ebenezer Howard's famous ideal of a
garden city. Thinking about the world we live in and how it
should look seems to be a deep instinct in human society. Perhaps it
arose when we stopped being nomads and started to build settlements.
Perhaps it was present even before then. Some accounts of planning
start with the city building of Ancient Greece and Rome. Planning is
seen as a kind of project management or architectural activity. Where
should the forum or market place go? How do we make housing
warm and sanitary? Shall we build city walls to make it secure?
And should they be round, square or pentangular? And indeed the
profession of planning began by emphasising the links to the other
professions of engineering and architecture.[2] But planning is both
more and less than this. Indeed it is a quite different kind of activity.

Focusing on planning as city-building puts far too much emphasis
on the way that our physical environment looks rather than how it
works, what we feel about it and how it was created. Planning is to be

found at the very centre of the complex mess of technology, politics, culture and economics that creates our urban society and its physical presence. In this book, I will explore how planning works, what it can do and what it cannot. I will try to answer the question of why we have planning systems and suggest why planning is important. I will show how we have a vital, even visceral relationship to what planning is all about. Planning is not the all-powerful process of shaping our cities. But it does tap into a really important part of our lives.

To start this exploration, it is worthwhile thinking about why it seems that human society needs planning. Why can't towns and cities just be left to themselves? The answer to this question lies in the way that towns and cities grow and change.

How towns and cities grow and change

By and large, cities have grown by their own devices. They have developed incrementally, adding bit by bit to the urban fabric. Where the additions are old enough, it can even look as if they have grown organically. And indeed, for most settlements, there is no overall master plan. Urban areas have grown as a result of many, largely uncoordinated actions by many different people and organisations. Let's look at some examples.

In 18th-century rural England, a wealthy family decides to build a house in the midst of their landholdings. The house is extended in several phases, until it becomes a small complex of buildings spreading out into the surrounding area. It becomes a focal point for the social activities of the local gentry and the economic life of the rural working classes. The local hamlet becomes a village and then a small town. Then the house's dominance in the area wanes with the growth of the industrial economy and nearby cities. Soon after the start of the 20th century, estate taxes and the decimation of the younger generation in World War One result in the break up of the estate into multiple ownerships. Part of the land is developed as housing, extending the town further. The farmland passes into other hands. The house falls into disrepair. But another century passes and the house finds a new life as a hotel, conference centre and spa, with some of the adjoining farmland having been turned into a golf course for visitors and residents in the executive housing estate at the edge of the town.

Over in 18th-century Continental Europe, in Germany, an artisan builds a machinery workshop for his small business. As the business grows over the next century, the workshop is added to and then demolished to make way for a succession of factories until a multi-story edifice dominates the town. The business is also the dominant source of employment in the town and, to house his workers, the industrialist (as he is now) has built a few streets of tenements. The workers from these and surrounding streets of somewhat meaner housing stream into the factory at regular intervals, while the noise and smoke is a continuous reminder of the industrial activities within. By the end of World War Two, part of the factory lies in ruins, burnt out and bomb-damaged. But a new modern factory rises phoenix-like from these ashes and new housing replaces many of the 19th-century homes. The renaissance doesn't last more than 50 years though. Competition from the Far East has put the factory out of business and it stands empty awaiting redevelopment. Most of the postwar housing is very run-down but the model tenements of the mid-19th century are now home to professionals, although few of their original residents would recognise the interiors.

Zola tells a fascinating story about how a department store grows from humble beginnings in Paris in his book *Au Bonheur Des Dames*.[3] Starting as a typical 19th-century draper's shop, the ambitious owner takes over neighbouring shops with the collaboration of a financier and creates a mammoth emporium. He negotiates new street building and literally undermines the one small umbrella seller in his block who refuses to sell out. All around, the older small shops are put out of business and can only look on as the armies of shop-workers and customers flow in and out of the new shopping palace. But change comes even to such palaces. Some of Zola's stores are still to be found in Paris, surviving on tourist and top-end retailing. But they face competition now, from shopping opportunities to be found across the city and often at lower cost. Retail malls, reached by car rather than foot, horse-drawn omnibus or Metro, are found on the urban outskirts, while shopping centres across the city increasingly house global brands.

—

Take one final example, a residential street in what is now downtown in an American city. The street has remained largely unchanged since it was built over a century ago. The houses are still recognisable from that time. But the dozens of people who have lived in No. 24 in the street could tell a different story. This house has moved from being a single family house to being split up into flats for working families to being a bed-and-breakfast hotel for a time. It has spent years empty, been vandalised for a while and then been home to a group of squatters. Its fortunes have followed those of the surrounding city. In recent years, downtown has become the fashionable place to live rather than a near-slum. No. 24 was bought up by a group of friends who were looking for a property development opportunity. They did the place up and sold it off as small studio flats, with a gym in the basement. More recently though, several of the singles who bought the flats have become couples and then families; families who often debate if they should stay in the downtown they love, with its restaurants and bars, or move to the suburbs with its green spaces and good schools.

These vignettes have been drawn from the urban history of the industrialised Northern hemisphere over the last two to three centuries. The scale and the pace of urban change will have varied over time and in different places. At times there would be incremental, almost imperceptible change; at others, the pace of change would have been faster than local communities could cope with, sweeping whole parts of cities into decline or redevelopment. And while these are tales of the global North, the essential story of urban change could apply to Mumbai, Tokyo or Cape Town. The message is that urban change has its own dynamics, resulting in continuous patterns of growth and decline.

These dynamics ultimately arise from the desire of individuals, companies and other kinds of organisation to pursue their interests, whether financial reward, status, comfort, survival or dreams of immortality. Their ability to do so will depend on their power, including economic and political power. Therefore, many commentators have argued that our cities reflect the power structures in society.[4] Those with money or political power will be the main driving forces in these patterns of urban change. This is partly why the outcomes of change are not always desirable from the perspective of society as a whole. These unacceptable consequences of urban growth and decline are the reasons why planning is considered necessary.

Why towns and cities can't be left to themselves

Our examples of urban change can also give us an insight into why such change generates demands for planning.

The urban history of the ancestral home in rural England might sound like a success story – a new use for a valued old building. But without planning, the redevelopment of the house as a hotel might destroy many valued historic features of that building. The surrounding landscape has already been altered by its transformation into a golf course; a land use with little space for natural habitats among its manicured greens; a water-hungry land use in an area that is already suffering periodic droughts. Climate change forecasts suggest that these droughts will only become worse. Climate change campaigners are also worried about the level of car use in the area. This country town has very limited public transport and most people who have a car use it to get to work, to the shops, to school and so on. The hotel also has a large car park and at times the traffic to conferences and special events can clog up the local roads. The executive housing, of course, has garaging for two cars for each household, adding to the value of the houses. Yet in the town there is a hidden homelessness problem. With limited social housing and given the high price of the private sector housing in the area, young people are squeezing into their parents' houses in multi-generation households or they are leaving the area and moving away.

Over in Germany, visitors to the city are struck by the ugly postwar development and the derelict buildings that remain in what is otherwise an attractive city. The benefits of development in the centre of the city don't seem to have spread out to this old industrial area. Residents of the 20th-century housing estates, once heralded as highlights of architectural modernism, find them difficult to live in. There is graffiti and vandalism. A lack of social facilities means that young people hang around the streets and courtyards, to the annoyance of many. High rates of local unemployment swell the numbers with adults as well, and the estate is increasingly becoming the venue for illicit activities such as drug dealing. Inside the houses, residents complain of mould and the high cost of heating. Lack of insulation and inefficient heating systems make these some of the most energy-guzzling buildings in the city. And while the old factories may no longer be working, they have left a legacy of pollution and waste. The river running through the area is sluggish and devoid of life. The professional residents of the refurbished 19th-century model worker housing are protected from all this. Their gated community has access out onto a road that skirts the housing and industrial estates and takes them straight into the city centre.

The beautiful old department stores in central Paris are still a tourist highlight. But the retail outlets elsewhere across the city, particularly towards the suburbs and on the outskirts, are rarely visited by tourists. These outlets provide a range of shopping and are well used, but they are accessible only by car, as evidenced by the acres of parking that surrounds each one. And it is difficult to distinguish one from another. Local residents wish that their local shopping centre felt just that – 'local' like French shopping used to be. They seem devoid of character, full of identical retailers selling identical products. There is no space for small local businesses any more; they cannot afford to pay the rents that the multiples do, given the prices that the multiples charge. There is little enough space to linger for shoppers either; the centres are just not designed for socialising, even during the day. And at night, they are closed down with gating to avoid a repeat of night-time antics by local gangs.

The by-now familiar tale of deprivation and wealth living cheek-by-jowl can also be told in New York. Only a few streets away from the gentrified downtown brownstones can be found families living in housing that has never been improved and remains haphazardly sub-divided into multiple dwellings. Here the downtown turns into inner-city, with its mobile population of students and recent migrants mixing with families who cannot afford to move anywhere else. Small businesses still exist here to serve the needs of this mixed community, albeit in rather ramshackle premises. But public services are severely limited and families have to take what they can get in the form of education and health services. The families that are increasingly found in the gentrified areas, however, are less willing to accept the existing state of public services. They complain about the lack of nursery school places and doctors' surgeries and the inability of the public services to keep pace with demographic change in the city. And all around the richer and poorer neighbourhoods, the endless flow of traffic in and out of the city pollutes the air and fills it with noise.

In each of these areas, urban change has resulted in loss – loss of buildings, of townscapes, of landscapes – as well new development. Some of these losses will be mourned while some will be welcomed as a way out of poverty and lack of opportunities. Urban change and economic development have always gone hand in hand as the main means of generating wealth. But when this wealth arrives, it is never evenly distributed and usually comes with unwanted side-effects – pollution, waste, noise and congestion, to name a few.

Planning has arisen in response to political pressure over the opportunities, losses and inequalities associated with urban change. Such pressure may come from many sources. Where there is money to be made from urban change, there will be pressure to promote it, to push for more development in particular locations and to increase the pace as well as scale of such development. And there will be others, less economically powerful, who will look to such development to provide the economic opportunities and social facilities that will give them a better, perhaps just a decent, life. Even the better off will still hope for development to bring more services, more attractive towns and cities, and better ways of urban living.

But then there will be those who feel threatened by such development, by the loss of valued parts of the environment – buildings, streets, landscapes. And there will be the communities and ways of life that would be destroyed along with the buildings, streets and fields. These may be middle-class communities resisting other groups moving into and changing their comfortable, settled lifestyles. Or they may be communities living at the margins of economic survival, who look to their neighbours and local small businesses to help support them.

And beyond these local pressures for planning, there are the pressure groups campaigning, as they see it, on behalf of society or the environment as a whole. These groups will be concerned about the extent to which urban life or urban change is threatening our common historic heritage and the environmental systems that sustain us. Traditionally these groups have sought to protect natural habitats and landscapes. Increasingly they talk of enhancing biodiversity and changing lifestyles to protect the climate.

There is no shortage of pressures for planning to protect, enhance and develop our towns and cities. These pressures have been evident for as long as urban areas have been growing and changing. The faster the pace of change, the greater those pressures tend to be. Planning systems across the world have been formed as a response to such pressures. But, as should be clear, these are multiple and often conflicting pressures. It is not possible to satisfy them all at the same time. How can planning systems cope with these demands and what is it reasonable to expect a planning system to do?

The role of planning

After such a litany of problems, it is tempting to see planning as the solution. And indeed it has often been presented as such – the guarantor of a desirable environment within which we can live and work to our full potential. Master planners, as the name implies, have often wanted to see themselves as a kind of urban superman, righting wrongs and creating the ideal city. The language here is deliberate as this is overwhelmingly a male planning and architectural fantasy. If there is a single message of this book, it is that this is a mistaken view of planning. Planning is not a panacea for all urban ills.

Rather, the answer to the question of "Why plan?" involves three debates. The first is about what a society wants from urban change. The second concerns the legitimate role of government vis-à-vis private interests. And the third is about the limits of the government's ability to deliver on society's expectations.

As our vignettes have outlined, urban change brings with it a host of different impacts, for good or ill. These impacts generate pressure on the political system for planning, pressures that are both positive and negative in relation to urban change. There will be pressures pushing for the promotion of urban change to deliver private wealth and public benefit, and there will be others trying to resist aspects of

–

urban change because of private harm and public costs. Housebuilders will be arguing for the planning system to allocate more housing land when the market is buoyant and there are profits to be made. Local residents in the vicinity will object to the loss of their views (and property values) and environmental pressures groups – such as the Sierra Club in the US or the Council for the Protection of Rural England – will object to the loss of landscape, countryside and habitats.

Choosing between different scenarios for the future is a complex business. It involves imagination as to what could possibly be achieved as well as practical judgement over what can actually be achieved. It involves debates between people and organisations to discuss critical choices about alternative development paths with different impacts. And it involves understanding these impacts and identifying impacts that might otherwise go unconsidered. But the central political problem is that the impacts of urban change fall variably on different people, groups and organisations. This is a key debating point. If one group benefits from development of this urban area, but at the cost of another group, what should society decide about this development? Are there trade-offs that should be made? Do some impacts count more than others? And are there ways that urban change could be managed to generate some compensation for the expected impacts?

Take the issue of development in areas liable to flooding. Perhaps surprisingly it is still possible to make profits by building and selling property in areas that are likely at some time to be flooded. Occupiers and owners, with the support of their insurance companies or without it, seem willing to take the risk. Should planning prevent such development even if the new houses could be sold and would help fill an acknowledged housing shortage? The developers claim that each new house would be fully flood-proofed and could recover quickly from flooding episodes. What if the residential development would contribute to the regeneration of the broader area? Would the decision change, if it could be shown that development in the floodplain would increase flood risks elsewhere by limiting the capacity to accommodate flood waters? Perhaps some of the profits of the scheme could pay for extra flood defences elsewhere. And what if it was argued that the floodplain was an important habitat for plants and other species? Would that matter?

In practical situations, the answers to such questions will depend on who is involved in the debates. So planning is also about deciding whose voice should be heard in determining these issues and, ultimately, whose voice should count. Therefore, at the heart of planning are issues of democracy. In societies where representative democracy does not have a place, then the answer often boils down to how state actors take these decisions. Where elections are a defining moment in public life, then politicians may lead the debate. But increasingly there have been demands for the public at large and local communities in particular to be given a voice in these discussions. So planning becomes a public space in which democracy is defined in practice. It identifies which voices a society regards as having a right to be heard and, beyond that, to have a significant influence on the decisions that are actually taken and the urban change that occurs.

But planning is not just about building visions of the future. It is also about seeking to achieve those visions through a mix of measures. In order to do so, the power of government has to be exercised. This could involve regulation, taxation or the compulsory appropriation of land. It could involve direct provision of developments that the market is slow to supply. It could involve public subsidy, tax breaks or the allocation of lucrative public contracts to certain companies and developers. So planning is also about the legitimate role of the public sector, acting in the avowed public interest, to intervene in the rights of private households, private companies and private landowners.

Of course, decisions about who should have a say within planning will have a significant influence on what is seen as legitimate intervention. And behind both of these questions lies the bigger one of what kind of society is considered desirable, in political, social and economic terms. A society in which existing property owners have a strong say in planning policy and outcomes will result in a different kind of planning system to one where local communities have the dominant voice. Where regulation, controlled by an elite of bureaucrats and politicians, is strongly exercised over all development and property interests, the planning process will be different from that operating in a situation where the emphasis is on encouraging debate among as wide a range of stakeholders and interests as possible, even at the expense of coming to speedy conclusions.

These kinds of judgement also affect expectations of the planning system in terms of whether it is succeeding or failing. Since most societies have had some form of planning for centuries, urban change cannot be considered as completely distinct from planning. Planning is not just an intervention in processes of urban change; it is part of urban change. Public culture understands this because it frequently blames the planning system for the undesirable aspects of urban change. Of course, it has been easy to overestimate the significance of planning processes within the overall mix of dynamics that generate this change. And, as a result, planning systems and planners have often been blamed for outcomes which are only partially their responsibility.

Nevertheless, the state can fail in managing urban change. A vision for a town or city looking to the future can turn out to be inappropriate. It can fail to take account of the consequences of urban change, whether intended or otherwise. It can also fail to foresee change and plan for that change. The list of planning failures is a long one.[5] New Towns in the UK have been criticised for their poor design, their soulless town centres, their overreliance on the car and their descent into becoming dormitory satellites of bigger cities rather than self-contained towns. Public housing estates in France and the US, to mention just two cases, have been lambasted for their social imbalance, squalid conditions and lack of facilities, a travesty of the modernist ideals of their original plans. And, to take a current concern, is planning taking sufficient account of climate change impacts to ensure that urban environments will be resilient in the face of changed temperature, rainfall, storm patterns, soil moisture content and sea-levels?

It is tempting to argue that none of these failures should happen; that planning should occur efficiently and effectively. It is a professional occupation, after all, and the profession should deliver to high standards. However, this cannot be just a question of professional competency unless we go back to a view of planning as a master-planning exercise. Rather, if we accept that planning is an inherently political and democratic exercise, then the question becomes: what are the legitimate limits to society's expectations of planning? What

—

can we reasonably expect planning to achieve and what risks are outside the reasonable scope of a planning system?

How planning works

Planning is, therefore, a means by which society collectively decides what urban change should be like and tries to achieve that vision by a mix of means. The most obvious and direct method is where the public sector takes a direct role in urban change, in building developments itself. This has been a significant aspect of creating new neighbourhoods and towns and, in some societies, this is still a dominant form. But increasingly urban change is achieved through interaction between the public and private sectors, even in societies that are dominated by state activity overall. This is in large part because of the perceived failure of the public sector to deliver the kind of urban change that is actually desired. It is also down to the drain on the public purse from financing such direct development.

As a result planning usually has to adopt more indirect means of achieving desired urban change. These are ways of persuading, encouraging and incentivising the private sector to provide new development of the desired type and in the desired location. One way of achieving this is through using public landownership but then getting the private sector to undertake the development. By controlling which sites are released for development, the public sector can exercise some control over the location and the pace of development. It can also use its position as landowner to negotiate the terms on which land is passed over to the developer and this can include detailed requirements about the type of development. In Sweden and the Netherlands it used to be a key aspect of housing policy that the local authorities had land banks, which they released to developers subject to conditions about the quality of housing or the prices at which the houses would be sold.[6]

However, if the final development is to be sold or let in the market-place, then financial viability remains a concern, even with public land provision. If the buildings cannot generate sufficient profit for the developer, then they won't get built, regardless of who is providing the land. Of course, the public sector can provide the land at lower cost; in effect, they are giving a subsidy to the development. This was a major reason why the development of London's Docklands in the early 1980s was so effective.[7] The land there was historically in the ownership of the Port of London Authority, which ran the docks. Under legislation, the land passed into the ownership of the London Docklands Development Corporation, whose main role was then to encourage commercial and residential development of the area by providing land at low prices.

Another way that the state can influence development activity is through building new infrastructure.[8] Urban development relies on a whole host of infrastructure to be usable. Transport routes are needed to get to and from the development; energy and water supply networks provide essential resources to occupiers; urban drainage and sewerage take waste away; and today communication networks are seen as necessary to commercial and domestic life.

Some of this infrastructure is essential for contemporary urban development. It is possible to create totally self-sufficient developments – and there can be compelling arguments for increasing self-sufficiency in the name of sustainability – but most new development relies on the existing infrastructure networks. Indeed it could be argued that a town or city is defined by these networks and the interconnectedness of its development.[9] Certainly the ability to connect to such networks and the cost of such connections is a key element in the profitability of any scheme.

Building new infrastructure networks, expanding them into previously un-serviced areas, can also be a major inducement to new development. Many of the major urban areas have expanded along newly built routes within transport networks. Metroland, in north-west London, refers to a huge area of inter-war suburban housing that followed the line of the new Metropolitan urban railway, heading out into what was then countryside. The stations along this line quickly acquired small shopping streets from which a mass of residential streets then radiated. Land which had only agricultural value was transformed into urban land, worth many multiples more. There was plenty of development profit to spur the building activity, split between the rail company who had bought up much of the land along its line and the various housebuilders.

—

A more direct way to encourage development is to provide a financial inducement. These can come with strings to ensure that only a certain type of development or one in a certain location is encouraged. There are examples all over the world of zones where certain taxes do not apply in order to encourage various kinds of industrial and retail development.[10] In the UK a 100% relief from stamp duty – the tax payable on the sale of a property – was announced in 2007 for new housing that was zero-carbon (that is, no net carbon emissions from the use of the house) in a bid to encourage more zero-carbon residential developments.[11] Most social housing developments can only operate with a direct development subsidy to make them viable as they will be rented out at below-market rates.[12]

However, this can make it sound as if most urban change occurs outwith the context of fiscal measures and the application of taxes and subsidies. Rather, outside of the black market, we all live right in the middle of a mass of taxation and subsidy systems. The structure of these fiscal systems is a major determinant of urban change. If the value added tax on refurbishment is different to that for new build, as it is in the UK, then this will affect the balance of development activity. So adjusting these systems at the margin could be considered a form of planning. The ability of government below the nation state, say at state or regional or city level, to use such tools depends on the legal limits to their taxation and spending powers and these will vary from country to country.

The most apparent form of local planning activity – and the one that people and companies usually have the strongest views about – is the use of regulation to achieve the visions set out in planning documents. Some countries have a system of zoning at the heart of their planning regulation.[13] Where a development complies with the more or less detailed requirement of a zoning ordinance, then it can go ahead. Building codes can operate on a similar basis, controlling the most detailed aspects of design and construction. Other countries use discretionary regulation, whereby each proposal for urban development has to get specific permission. This system is called discretionary because there is always a degree of discretion in how and when that permission is granted. In the UK, regulation is of this kind but is supposed to be plan-led.[14] This means that planners should look

—

14

first of all at the agreed plans to decide if a development can proceed. However, there is still scope for judgement and for negotiation about the details of development. In particular, negotiation can be used to trade off the benefits and costs of a development against each other, to persuade the developer to provide additional compensatory benefits to balance off some negative impacts arising from the development. The term 'planning gain' is often used for such compensation.[15]

Some might argue that heavy negotiation during regulation should only be a fallback within planning. Rather the aim should be that developers come forward with development proposals that are acceptable to the planning system. Ideally the aim of the plans that planners create should be to communicate to everyone what the goals for urban change are, and all stakeholders should buy in to these goals. They are more likely to do so if they have been centrally involved in making those plans and deciding on those goals, and the process by which these plans are drawn up can be important in getting those involved in urban change to think along similar lines. But the inevitable conflicts between urban stakeholders over the impact of planning decisions make this less likely to happen and can constrain such consensual planning.

And finally, information and education has a place in the toolbox of planning measures. This is about changing the norms and expectations of what urban change should look like and how it will occur. For example, in the sustainability arena, there are now a mass of assessment schemes for new buildings (LEAD, BREEAM, and so on), which are ways of telling developers and occupiers what a sustainable building is, getting them to expect higher sustainability standards and produce more sustainable buildings.[16] The information contained in such assessments can be used by planners to influence urban change.

All these means of planning are potentially controversial. They use public funds and they are often seen as interfering with private rights. Not everyone benefits equally from the outcomes of planning and some will feel this keenly. There are often substantial profits to be made from the use of these tools and approaches, and where this is the case the pressures for influence on the planning system are intense. Planning is controversial and the contested nature of planning processes, debates, decisions and outcomes is the subject of this book.

—

The rest of the book

The rest of the book explores the way that the planning system pursues its purpose. It begins, in Chapter Two, by looking at the 'big picture', the way that strategic plans are developed and how they work, as well as the problems involved in creating such visions. Chapters Three, Four and Five then go on to discuss three tasks that the planning system takes on: the allocation of land for housing, urban regeneration and conservation of both built and natural heritage. Chapter Six considers the issues surrounding the involvement of the public in planning decision-making, particularly around opposition to development proposals, and Chapter Seven looks at the conflicts between the planning system and households wishing to develop their own property. Finally, Chapter Eight draws together the key themes of the book and looks at the question of how planning can deliver the good life, understood in terms of sustainable towns and cities.

TWO

The big picture

Planning implies having a plan – the big picture – but this plan can take different forms and be achieved in different ways. This chapter is about the process of developing a plan and the kinds of plan that results. And what are the complexities of developing such a big picture? Planning has been subject to much criticism for its grand visions and its slow, complicated plan-making processes. People can point to outcomes in our urban environments that are less than ideal: persistent problems of inadequate housing; housing estates without proper transport provision and lacking retail and social facilities; town centres that could never work because of the lack of infrastructure; areas of urban decline with poor quality of the public realm; loss of valued features of the urban environment. Why hasn't planning provided a big picture to address these problems effectively? Many of these issues will be addressed in later chapters but here the central question of how planning produces a plan is tackled. How does planning take the bigger view and provide a robust vision of how an area should change?

Producing a plan

Plans can take many different forms and come in many different guises. In the UK, plans have been called development plans, comprehensive development area plans, local plans, structure plans, action area plans, unitary development plans, regional spatial strategies and, most recently, local development plan documents (such as a core strategy or an area action plan) and supplementary planning documents as part of a local development framework. In addition there are plans for distinct policy areas within or touching on planning such as transport, waste management, minerals, conservation of built heritage, landscape protection, national parks, biodiversity, climate

—

protection and so on. Some of these plans are long, extending to hundreds of pages; some take up only a few pages. Some are mainly text; some mainly comprise a map.

What all these documents have in common is that they provide a vision of how an area or an aspect of that area will change into the future. They are all outputs of a planning process, a generic process that is trying to think about the locality and options for change. However, there have been different models of this generic process over time.[1] Planning as a contemporary activity has modernist roots, which have influenced the way it operates, the kinds of plans that have been produced, the urban aesthetics that have been espoused and the identity of planners.[2]

Modernist planning as a process is characterised by aspirations to a comprehensive approach, taking all factors into account in devising the plan. It assumes a great deal of prior knowledge about current situations and future trends, as well as command over the means of implementing the plan. As a result, the planner is imbued with authority, expertise and control and the public sector is granted status, power and ultimate responsibility with regard to urban change. The scope of such a modernist planning approach is apparently unlimited. However, experience has shown that its ambition has tended to outstrip its reach. Such planning suffers from a number of problems in the real world.[3]

The information that is available to planners is rarely sufficient fully to model current and alternative situations, and so assumptions and judgements have to be made about the key features of the locality at present and the options for change. Yet, at the same time, the information that is available often overloads the capacity of planners to decide between options in a rational manner. Instead there is a resort to judgement, influenced by established norms, patterns and expectations about future development paths. Prevailing views within planning circles (both professional and academic) of how areas are changing and what should be the appropriate way of responding shape the preparation of plans in practice, providing a shortcut through the laborious modernist process of 'survey, analysis and plan'[4].

In addition, the modernist assumption that planning authorities have sufficient means of implementing plans is often misplaced. The

—

pursuit of resources to implement the plan can end up shaping the plan itself, so that plan formulation and implementation become intermeshed rather than distinct stages of planning with the plan leading urban change.[5] In the worst cases, plan making has been a process of catching up with the development that has already occurred rather than leading future change; this was the experience in the 1960s in the UK when residential development outside of planned areas ran ahead of the ability of the planning system to devise up-to-date plans with new allocations for development areas.[6]

Finally, the modernist view of planning is an expert-led approach. It allows a role for political processes only in setting the goals for planning practice. Thus central and local politicians may determine whether an area should be pursuing growth or not, or broadly what kind of growth. But thereafter the devising of detailed plans for the type and location of growth is supposed to be the remit of the professional, expert planner. However, the reality is that political pressures remain a key influence on planning decisions at national and local levels all the way through the planning process, from broad goals, to consideration of options, choice of strategy and implementation via decisions about specific developments. The stated goals of planning often get revised and restated during this process; goal setting, policy formulation and implementation are thus all continuously interrelated through the planning process and are all highly politicised. This undermines modernist claims for the role of expertise within planning.

In response to these criticisms of the modernist model of planning, a rather different model has emerged in which planning is about integration and joined-up thinking in the development of a vision for an area. Central to this is the involvement of multiple stakeholders. Modernist planning sought to internalise different perspectives within the planning process and furthermore within the planning organisation, usually the local authority planning department. It was the remit of the planning system to collect all the necessary information, to consider all the costs and benefits of a situation, to plan from all possible angles and come up with the optimal outcome. The responsibility and glory, but also the blame, for outcomes from modernist planning then rested with the planners and ultimately the

—

failure of modernist planning arose from the trail of poor planning outcomes that were giving planners a bad name.

The alternative model of planning takes a quite different approach, seeing the planner in the midst of a web of contacts, who are all working together to produce the plan. It involves recognising the inability of the planning system to fulfil its goals on its own because the public sector (and specifically the planning authority) has only limited power, capacities and resources. Planning needs the power, capacity and resources of other parts of the public sector, namely agencies and authorities at different scales of government and those dealing with other policy domains. It also needs the power, capacity and resources of the private sector.

The general paradigm that covers such planning is one of governance.[7] Governance works by creating networks, sometimes described as semi-autonomous and self-regulating. This means that these networks have a degree of separation from central and local government; they are not departments or divisions of those authorities. And they have some control over how they operate and regulate their behaviour. Under conditions of governance, planning is not the work of the planner or even the planning department. Rather, planning arises from the actions of networks that have a separate identity, a specific task and even a responsibility to deliver on certain public goals. Planning networks thus exist as separate entities but are always linked back to planning authorities in the public sector; they are only semi-autonomous. They work out their own modes of operation to deliver the plans that they want and they have to find a way of being sustainable, at least until their goals are delivered or abandoned.

The late 20th and early 21st centuries have seen a proliferation of such networks, usually under the name of partnerships or assemblies or some more creative moniker. In England, the Local Strategic Partnerships (LSPs) that exist within local authorities are one such governance network. These LSPs have been established to represent those organisations with a key stake in the local area. For example, in Birmingham, Be Birmingham describes itself as "the local strategic partnership for Birmingham that brings together partners from the business, community, voluntary, faith and public sectors to deliver a

—

better quality of life in Birmingham".[8] It is actually based on a "family of partnerships" or a network of networks, with seven Thematic Partnerships and a Neighbourhoods Board. Be Birmingham organises summits three times a year with a wider level of participation by outside organisations, but it is run by an executive board with senior city council officers sitting alongside representatives from all the Thematic Partnership boards and key external agencies concerned with local economic development, employment, training, voluntary services, health services, fire services and policing. LSPs such as Be Birmingham are responsible for preparing and overseeing the implementation of the Sustainable Community Strategy, which is the key strategic plan for the local authority.

Under governance, a similar approach is taken to devising and delivering plans for urban change. A wide range of stakeholders, including, but not only, local communities, will be involved in consultation on planning documents. For example, as of March 2010, Birmingham City Council were consulting on their Core Strategy, two Area Action Plans, two Conservation Area management plans, an urban rivers and floodplains sustainable management plan and plans for works to a major open space, Weoley Castle Square. In addition, the stakeholder network of the LSP will have an influence. As the council sets out in its Statement of Community Involvement:

> Our planning policies should reflect the objectives of the Community Strategy, and to assist this the BSP [Birmingham Strategic Partnership] has agreed a series of principles which will be used to guide the process of preparing land use plans. By working closely with the Birmingham Strategic Partnership and any other groups flowing from the Sustainable Community Strategy the Council will ensure that the Local Development Framework is closely integrated with the Sustainable Community Strategy.[9]

At the regional scale, regional assemblies have brought together regional stakeholders under public sector leadership to prepare regional spatial strategies. Under the new coalition government's plans to abolish regional spatial strategies, this will be replaced by private sector-led Local Enterprise Partnerships to provide the regional vision. While the leadership and perhaps some of the partnership composition may differ, this is just another example of governance at work at the regional scale.

Thus postmodernist planning involves considerable work of engagement with a variety of groups as a priority. This has been captured in an influential planning theory, known as collaborative planning, championed by Patsy Healey.[10] Drawing on Habermasian social theory, collaborative planning focuses on the way that the different people and organisations involved in debates about urban change communicate with each other. Seeing the potential for consensus as inherent within the act of communication, it assesses the extent to which this potential is frustrated by the way communication is carried out in practice and the exercise of power by different organisations. Planners are charged with handling communication between stakeholders so that their relative power does not determine the course of planning discussions and outcomes. The aim is to have communication that enables the different parties to understand each other's point of view and come to an agreement. Hopefully this agreement will be one that all parties can buy into or at least accept and one that moves beyond any conflicts between those parties. Within collaborative planning, the aim is to release the potential of communication to deliver agreements, hopefully a form of consensus but at least a mutually acceptable compromise.

Planning and land uses

So the process of plan making has moved from a modernist approach, which sees the planner as the rational author of the plan, to one which emphasises the involvement of stakeholders in communication with each other. But where does this leave the form of the plan that results?

One of the earliest rationales for planning was to plan the different uses of land so as to promote local well-being and economic prosperity. Initially the emphasis was on avoiding the inappropriate juxtaposition of incompatible land uses. In particular the location of housing in proximity to industrial areas was seen as a public health

—

threat and the emblem of an irrationally planned city. Separation of land uses became the standard way of preventing these different uses of land impacting negatively on each other. Thus if a shopping area was going to attract lots of traffic, it was better to place it on a road interchange and away from residential areas so that families would not be affected by the traffic. Industrial areas continued to be located away from other land uses for similar reasons, together with any pollution fears.

This essentially negative approach to locating different land uses was supplemented by the argument that a well-planned city would have different land uses located so that they positively reinforced each other. This would mean putting green spaces next to residential areas, planning the location of schools so that they served nearby family housing, placing offices near to railway stations and shopping centres near to bus interchanges, and so on. In economic jargon, this is termed maximising positive externalities of land use and minimising negative externalities.[11]

This approach also meant creating clusters of similar land uses where each occupier would benefit from proximity to the others. Thus offices would benefit from being in a distinct office district since support services for the office sector would grow up in the area, attracted by the larger market. There would also be possibilities for the different office occupiers to supply each other and to benefit from face-to-face contact in the business district. The same arguments apply to industrial firms clustering together in an industrial park, while retail outlets benefit from the larger customer flow that is attracted to a collection of shops in a retail park, shopping mall or shopping centre. Again using economists' jargon, this concentration of land uses allows agglomeration economies to be generated.[12]

The evidence for the efficiency of planning in concentrating, separating and juxtaposing approach land uses would, according to this view, be found in the pattern of land values. The planning system could foster a pattern of land uses that minimises negative spillover effects like pollution (that is, the negative externalities), maximises the positive spillover effects like the benefits of public space (that is, the positive externalities) and fosters agglomeration economies arising from clustering. This should result in the value of the land

—

being increased beyond the baseline of what would have occurred in the absence of planning. The rational planning of land uses through the planning system would thus increase land values.

This kind of thinking has underpinned the spatial patterning of new development in many planning documents. Zoning is the clearest example, but more indicative plans still tend to identify where new development should go by the clear delineation of areas for different land uses. More importantly, the form of urban areas has been shaped by this approach. Towns and cities tend to have areas devoted to different land uses. Some theorists have modelled this as a 'natural' phenomenon, arising from social and economic dynamics.[13] Urban sociologists have drawn diagrams identifying the central business district, the transition zone, suburbs, and so on. They suggest that there are processes of growth, invasion and succession of different land uses in these zones that explain urban change. Urban economists have come up with rather similar diagrams, explaining the pattern of land use in terms of competition between different land uses for sites, with land going to the use that can bid the highest price. By working with these sociological and economic processes, the planning system reinforces the separation of land uses and at the margin even creates it.

However, almost a century of experience with the planned ordering of land uses has suggested significant problems with this approach. Principally, under conditions of urban growth, the concentration and separation of land uses has led to an overall increase in the amount of travel within the city.[14] Since most of this travel is being undertaken by car, the result has been significant problems of congestion, air pollution and greenhouse gas emissions. A further problem is that monofunctional areas tend to have activity during only part of the day. This contributes to rush-hour traffic patterns and means that large parts of the city – industrial, commercial and retail areas – are socially dead for many hours. This can foster antisocial behaviour during the downtimes, when such behaviour goes undetected by routine forms of social surveillance.

Thus current thinking favours a more mixed pattern of land use (except where industrial pollution concerns persist). By putting different land uses close to each other in a more finely grained urban

—

pattern, the hope is that this will reduce the need to travel long distances and create the potential for using non-motorised means (that is, cycling and walking). The city would also be more vibrant, with active social life on more streets throughout the day and into the evening. Some of this has been captured in the vision of New Urbanism as an urban design and planning paradigm.[15]

However, the main problem with developing a planning vision based on land uses is that it merely describes the desired pattern of land uses. There is nothing inherent in the plan that suggests the process by which this pattern will arise. The assumption is that the publication of a document based around a land use pattern will provide information about how the future will pan out and a framework for the development and investment decisions of key urban stakeholders. There is usually a reliance on regulatory processes to back this up but, as we will see in later chapters, such regulation is highly dependent on market dynamics and community engagement for its outcomes.

This has led to calls for a different kind of plan, arising out of a process that is based in governance processes and ideas of collaborative planning, that is, spatial planning. Spatial planning not only emphasises stakeholder engagement but also is based on the idea of integrating policies across different tiers of government and different policy sectors through such engagement. In Europe the face of the spatial planning approach is the European Spatial Development Perspective (ESDP), adopted in 1999.[16] This complex plan highlighted both forms of integration, arguing that "Spatial development issues in the EU can, in future, only be resolved through cooperation between different governmental and administrative levels",[17] and also that "The ESDP provides the possibility of widening the horizon beyond purely sectoral policy measures, to focus on the overall situation of the European territory".[18]

Spatial planning also became the official face of planning in England and Wales under the Planning and Compulsory Purchase Act 2004. Integration through wide stakeholder engagement is at the heart of the new approach. As central government guidance, set out in Planning Policy Statement 12, states, spatial planning aims to:

—

- produce a vision for the future of places that responds to the local challenges and opportunities, and is based on evidence, a sense of local distinctiveness and community derived objectives, within the overall framework of national policy and regional strategies;
- translate this vision into a set of priorities, programmes, policies, and land allocations together with the public sector resources to deliver them;
- create a framework for private investment and regeneration that promotes economic, environmental and social well being for the area;
- coordinate and deliver the public sector components of this vision with other agencies and processes.[19]

In order to achieve this, spatial planning necessarily implies a particular focus on infrastructure provision and investment.

The importance of infrastructure

As Chapter One outlined, appropriately planned infrastructure systems are essential for functional urban development. The occupiers of development need access to energy, water, drainage, transport and communications, and hence to physical networks of wires, pipes, rails and roads. But there is also the need for social infrastructure in the form of health, education and social support facilities. Planning can take a responsive approach to infrastructure provision, and in many cases has done so. That is, the planning system looks at the development that is taking place or is planned to take place and seeks to ensure that the necessary facilities and networks are in place to service that development. The danger with this approach is that the infrastructure is only patchily provided and hence poorly serviced development results. In addition the infrastructure that results may not be the most cost-effective or resource-efficient structure.

To avoid this, a more proactive approach is needed, one that looks to finance and plan the provision of infrastructure alongside or even before new urban development occurs. If the latter route is taken, then there is the prospect of actually shaping the pattern of new

—

development – where it goes and what it is like. As we shall see, this can be a way of making new urban development more sustainable.

Shaping transport infrastructure has long been recognised as a way to lead urban development. In the 19th and early 20th centuries, the opening of new rail lines was influential in shaping the pattern of urban growth. With the arrival of the household car, some of this potential has been lost because the use of road networks is so much more spatially diffuse and difficult to control. However, much blame must also be laid at the door of transport planners. Planning of transport infrastructure has tended to be defined by a supply-led logic, assuming that the road networks should be expanded again and again in response to greater car ownership and more road travel.[20] New urban development, particularly on the periphery or outside established areas, then followed on such road improvements, since they created more capacity for car travel and hence enhanced accessibility.

Such expansion of the road network and associated road traffic has been a major source, and furthermore a growing source, of greenhouse gas emissions. In 2004 transport accounted for 27% of the UK's carbon dioxide emissions, mainly from road transport; this had increased by 10% from 1990.[21] The climate-change agenda therefore presents a major challenge to this approach of predicting the demand for road use and then supplying road space. Instead, there has been a call for the demand for transport and in particular road use to be managed; the so-called 'new realism' in transport planning.[22] This approach puts the planning system in a very different position.

In a predict-and-provide world, the planning system would work out how much development will be needed for social and economic reasons and then analyse the implications for the road network. New roads would be planned and built with urban development fitting into the new road network. Instead, under a climate-change agenda, the emphasis is on deciding where the development should go in order to reduce the need to travel and the demand for road transport. This has led to planning approaches that increase the density of development and encourage development within existing urban areas, on the basis that low density urban sprawl and rural developments are more likely to increase road traffic.[23]

Alongside this attempt to plan for less travel has gone a parallel attempt to ensure that more travel uses less carbon-intensive transport modes. Public transport – whether bus, guided bus, tram or rail – and non-motorised modes – cycling and walking – become the favoured modes. This again has implications for planning. Increasing the take-up of public transport requires attention to the routes served but also many other details of public transport planning, such as frequency of the service, the comfort and perceived social status of the rolling stock, the information provided to travellers, the fare structure and the ease of changeover between routes and services. Meanwhile, planning for cycling and walking puts the emphasis on the detail of urban design to create safe and attractive routes for cyclists and pedestrians.[24]

Planning can play a similar role in relation to infrastructure networks for energy and water (both supply and disposal).[25] Such networks have tended to be both extensive and centralised but this need not be the case.[26] Rather, the tendency towards large networks and centralised management is a feature of how infrastructure providers have viewed the problem and established ways of handling service delivery and waste removal. So energy has been generated in centralised locations and then distributed through national grids, which provide gas or electricity to households and firms across the country whenever they want to use it. Locations which do not have access to such grids of power and fuel have been viewed as deprived of a central feature of modern life.

Similarly, water supply has tended to focus on the capture of water resources through reservoirs and pumping stations or even desalination plants in certain locations and the flow of water through pipes to development locations. As development areas grow, so more water has to be found and transported around the country. Clean water is fundamental to public health and hence such water supply is seen as a basic right. Its supply is also linked in to the adequacy of the drainage systems, taking away polluted water from households and firms and also from urban surfaces; this includes so-called 'grey' water as well as 'black' water or sewage. Separating this dirty water from sources of clean water is essential to maintaining public health and this has led to investment in two distinct networks (clean and

—

28

waste water) and in water treatment so that the polluted water can be recycled back into water courses, allowing for further abstraction.

Extending the geographical range of such energy, water and drainage networks removes a key constraint to development in specific locations. Development on a site without access to these networks has generally been regarded as inappropriate. This has put the emphasis on making sure that a modern, developed country is fully networked with regard to water and energy. However, networks that serve larger areas and more developments need more capacity. As there is more urban development, so the pressure grows for more investment in power stations, reservoirs and water treatment plants. A logical cycle emerges whereby centralised infrastructure networks and urban development have to grow together. To do anything else is seen as poor planning.

There is beginning to be a rethink about some of this logic. As with transport infrastructure, a focus on the sustainable use of resources has challenged this 'supply-on-demand' approach and put more emphasis on the management of demand for energy and water. It can make economic as well as environmental sense to promote greater energy efficiency rather than simply expand the capacity for energy generation. Similarly, water efficiency measures may be both more economic and sustainable than increasing water supply capacity.

The sustainability agenda has also challenged the idea of energy and water networks necessarily being dominated by centralised systems. Increasingly the role of decentralised energy generation and distribution is being championed, particularly as this can harness renewable energy sources, may increase the efficiency of energy generation and distribution and engage local communities more fully in energy demand management. Combined heat and power plants, district heating schemes, micro- or meso-generation from renewable sources are all examples of this challenge to centralised energy networks.[27]

In terms of water systems, the potential of recycling water within a building or development site is being emphasised. Separation of grey and black water within a building allows the grey water to be deployed for uses where drinking water quality is not essential (such as toilet flushing). On a site basis, there may be potential for rush-beds to clean grey and even black water for re-use. Water capture on a more localised basis, with relevant treatment, can supply some water needs. And in terms of drainage, rather than all waste water automatically being piped away for centralised treatment and disposal, sustainable urban drainage systems are being seen as ways of dealing with drainage demands more locally.[28]

These changes in thinking are all shifting the emphasis of infrastructure planning away from the big picture of building centralised networks towards enabling buildings and development areas to make more use of decentralised energy supply and localised water supply and treatment. Energy and water planning then becomes integrated into urban design and planning rather than being the context within which such development design and planning fits. A similar trend can also be seen in relation to drainage and waste management. The emphasis is increasingly on dealing with the problem of solid waste and waste water disposal in or near the development through waste reduction, recycling and even treatment. Solid waste can feed into local energy-from-waste systems for generating energy, and waste water can become part of local blue infrastructure systems of ponds, swales and rills, being cleaned through reed beds and contributing to local biodiversity and visual amenity.

The role of social infrastructure should not be forgotten in this focus on environmental sustainability. To be socially sustainable, a development needs access to good schools, health clinics and other social services as well as commercial facilities for shopping and leisure activities and non-profit community centres, including places of worship. Some of these are provided by the private sector and hence the scale of provision is dependent on the level of demand rather than need; this can affect the scale and quality of retail facilities in an area. But other services are provided by the public sector and thus there is the potential for matching the scale of public investment in these services to the needs arising from urban development. In the past there has tended to be a disconnect between urban development planning and social infrastructure planning. Often social service providers have to play catch-up by providing facilities after the needs of residents become apparent. Spatial planning is seeking to change this by placing the planning of public sector investment in social and other infrastructure more centrally within the overall planning of urban change. The key questions are whether and how it is able to achieve this goal.

The limits to spatial planning

So planning is about coordination and integration. It is about looking at all the different aspects of urban development to decide whether and where it should be permitted. It is about considering all the different dimensions of urban development to create something that will really enhance a local area and contribute to sustainability. It is about thinking of all the different needs of, and opportunities for, an area in order to guide where new infrastructure investment should go. It is about taking as comprehensive a view as possible by engaging with relevant stakeholders.

However, taking this broad, comprehensive view is very difficult. It involves not only cognitive ability but also, more prosaically, time and resources. This is because coordination between different actors and integration of their different plans requires the building of many links between actors and between plans. The more people and organisations are involved, the more links are needed and the greater the planning effort. Often these links are operating across sectoral boundaries, where organisations with very different kinds of interest and motivation are involved. Often they occur across different spatial scales. Infrastructure planning requires the involvement of key stakeholders at the local, regional and national scales, since even decentralised systems usually need to connect to regional and national systems.[29]

However, spatial planning is intended to be more than just the integration of the diverse elements required to make urban development work effectively and sustainably. It is also intended to be proactive rather than reactive. The discussion above has emphasised how to make infrastructure planning more proactive so that it leads urban development. But the idea of spatial planning is also about being more proactive in relation to the urban development itself. One of the key criticisms of both zoning systems and the dual system of

—

development planning and development control that characterises the UK planning system is that they depend on other organisations coming forward with development proposals that the planning system then reacts to. It may be that part of the public sector initiates the development proposal – say the housing department or an urban regeneration agency – but in general the main source of development proposals that the planning system has to deal with come from the private sector.

There are only a limited number of ways that the planning system can influence these proposals, as Chapter One has discussed. Spatial planning puts the emphasis on the involvement of key stakeholders in the planning process to deliver planned investment and, for those not directly involved in these discussions, the identification of suitable locations for development in plans. This is a form of indicative planning but it can be a rather weak form of planning. There is no requirement for the private sector or even public sector agencies to take such suggestions seriously. Doing so may reduce the time spent on processing any necessary permissions for development, but if an organisation owns other potential development sites, then it will always be in their interests to try and push against the signals sent by indicative planning to get permission for their land. Only if there is virtually no scope for getting development permission outside of such indicative land allocations does indicative planning then have more power. Removing the right to appeal against a refusal of permission when the proposal goes against indicative allocations (as suggested in the UK Conservative Party's green paper on planning)[30] would increase planners' power here.

As previously discussed, spatial planning seeks to overcome the limitations of indicative planning by using infrastructure provision as a way to lead development activity. By integrating this with a full consideration of the range of service and infrastructure provision, the result should be a more planned form of urban change. The question is how effective spatial planning can be, particularly in bringing infrastructure providers and developers into planning discussions. The reason why such interests would be willing to be involved in such arrangements is twofold. First, they thereby hope to facilitate the process of achieving development permissions for their projects, either on sites they hold or on sites that they learn through the spatial planning process will be preferred for development. But second, spatial planning works where stakeholders are reassured as to the value of investing time and resources in such discussions by the planning system's overt commitment to facilitating development. The proactive nature of spatial planning is thus also a pro-development stance.

The intention of the shift to spatial planning is that planning should no longer be seen as a restrictive bureaucratic exercise that constrains development and, thereby, adversely affects the economy and the possibilities for urban change. Rather, it puts a more development-friendly attitude at the heart of planning and then seeks to shape the nature of that development. An important implication is that this justifies reducing the scope for consultation and, in particular, objections within the overall process of generating plans for an area. In the UK version of spatial planning, such consultation is now front-loaded, meaning that it mainly occurs early on in the discussions about what local plans should look like. The question is how this will fare when faced with pressures for conservation and the involvement of local communities and the private interests of those opposed to further urban development. These are issues considered in Chapters Five and Six. But first the discussion of how to plan proactively for residential development and urban regeneration is taken forward in Chapters Three and Four.

—

THREE

Somewhere to lay my hat

Providing land allocations for new housebuilding (that is, for building for new dwellings, both houses and flats) is one of the key roles for a planning system. This chapter is about the pressures for new housebuilding and the need for planning to influence that building. It is also about the relationship of the planning system to the market dynamics that deliver most new housing. Is planning too strong or not strong enough? Can it deliver the kind of housing that society needs?

The need for housebuilding

Housing, of a decent quality and at an affordable price, is a basic human need. The right to 'a standard of living adequate for the health and well-being of himself and his family [sic]', specifically mentioning housing, is enshrined in Article 25 of the United Nations' Universal Declaration of Human Rights. However, we currently live in a world where many people are deprived of this right. Even in wealthy countries, access to decent and affordable housing is a problem. So one reason for building more housing is to meet this need.

This point is amplified if population growth is considered. The UN currently estimates the global population in 2010 at just over 6.9 billion and predicts it will grow to 8 billion by 2025, although longer-term trends are more uncertain.[1] Of course, this growth is not evenly spread across countries and regions. The most rapid growth is in Africa and Asia among the lower-middle income countries. North America will experience modest growth but Europe as a global region will decline from 729 million in 1999 to 701 million in 2025.

Changes in population figures are a result of natural change (births and deaths) and migration. While natural change occurs relatively slowly, migration can rapidly alter population figures at a national

—

scale. The UK currently experiences net in-migration, usually of 100,000–200,000 people per annum.[2] But given that planning operates at the regional and local levels, sub-national patterns of migration are a significant factor in considering housing need and the requirement for more housebuilding. For example, in the South East region of England, over 220,000 people moved into the area in the year ending April 2006.[3] And of course, as some regions grow, others may decline.

However, population figures are less relevant when considering housing than household numbers. Even in countries where the population is stable or declining, a societal shift towards smaller household size can mean that household numbers are growing, each household requiring a home. In the UK the number of households grew from just under 23 million in 1991 to almost 25 million in 2006, outstripping population growth and largely due to the growth of one-person households, particularly elderly one-person households.[4]

These patterns of household formation are in continuous flux. While an in-migrating group may favour living in large family groups, this can change over time as expectations alter in line with dominant social norms. Some larger households are reflections of the 'hidden homeless', whereby young families or young singles live with parents because they cannot find an affordable home of their own. Social change such as falling family size, the increasing incidence of chosen childlessness and divorce, together with greater longevity, all contribute to smaller households. But this may not mean more demand for smaller dwellings as shared childcare between separated parents requires space for the same children in more than one home and older households may also want space for family visitors.

These complex demographic and social pressures create housing need and charge the planning system with the responsibility of meeting this need with a sufficient housing stock. 'Sufficient' will mean a slight surplus as not all the houses can be considered genuinely available for occupation. Vacancies are needed in any housing system to allow for movement within the housing stock. Many countries have vacancy rates in excess of this; in the UK about 3% of the total stock is vacant.[5]

—

36

The lesson of all this arithmetic is that there is often a need for housebuilding to bring the aggregate figures for housing supply and need into some kind of balance. However, such total housing numbers hide a number of important issues regarding the fit between households and homes. Are all these houses of an adequate quality? Are they the right size? Are they in the places where people want to live? And are they affordable? Planning tries to address all these questions.

Slum clearance was one of the earliest justifications for planning activity. In the UK, there were periods of demolishing and replacing inadequate housing in the late 19th century and again following both World Wars. While many would criticise some of the replacement housing, the need to tackle unsanitary housing was unassailable. And such problems persist. In England, 7.7 million homes were assessed as not meeting 'decent housing' standards in 2007, amounting to just under 35% of the housing stock.[6] Upgrading these properties or replacing them with better new properties is essential.

The second question concerns the required size of individual dwellings. Even if there is enough decent housing stock, it can be of the wrong size distribution to fit the patterns of households emerging from demographic and social change. There might be scope to convert existing dwellings to make homes of the right size for the families in housing need. Small dwellings can become a large one and vice versa. Planning often exercises a degree of control over such conversions and subdivisions and this can be a way of creating a better balance between housing and family need. And, of course, planning can also influence the size of new homes built.

The third question concerns the location of existing housing. As the discussion of migration has emphasised, people are mobile; unfortunately most housing is not. So a mismatch can arise quite readily between where the people are and where the available homes are. Local planning has a primary role to play in redressing such imbalances by permitting new housebuilding and deciding where new housebuilding should occur; this will discussed further later in the chapter.

Finally, a question was posed about the affordability of housing. Here planning policy has to interface with the relative roles of the

—

market and the public sector in allocating housing to households and determining price or rental levels. How market processes influence the availability of housing, particularly new housing, is also discussed further below.

The amount of housebuilding

It is clear that there is no easy answer to the question of how much new housebuilding there should be.[7] A lack of decent, affordable houses in the right location means that some new residential development is required to meet the needs of demographic change and the ongoing deterioration of the existing housing stock. Indeed planning policy has tended to see such new development as the main means of solving the housing problem. This may be development on a clear site, refurbishment of existing buildings, conversion of such buildings or a mixture of all three. But how should the quantity of such development in a specific location be decided?

We can begin to explore this question by considering whether or not it could be left to market processes. The argument for a market-led approach runs as follow. The private sector makes its profits from supplying the demand for new housing. Where this demand exists, then it will act to fill the gap between the existing housing stock and the number of households needing housing. It will achieve this by building, refurbishing and converting buildings into smaller or larger units. These dwellings will then be bought for owner-occupation or by landlords for renting out.

The problems with this approach are several. First, the housebuilding industry responds to demand not need. This means that it builds primarily for those consumers with the ability to pay. While this is not always at the top end of the housing market, there will be a substantial sector of the population who do not have enough money available to rent or purchase at a price that makes for profitable residential development.

Second, the housebuilding industry tends to build in locations where it can obtain land at a price that makes the development profitable. Development profits come from the gap between the price of new housing and all the costs of developing that housing, including

—

the price paid for the land. For many housebuilders finding enough land at the right price is a significant constraint on their development activities. Sometimes developers may have a bank of land bought cheaply that they are keen to build out; as a result they put pressure on the planning system to permit development on such sites. For these reasons, new housing may not be in locations of housing need.

Those in favour of letting the market decide argue that the main constraint on developers getting access to land is the planning system, and that if the planning system was abolished, or at least relaxed, then the market would encourage landowners to sell their land to housebuilders. Furthermore, the price at which landowners would sell would reflect the demand for housing and not an artificial restriction of supply; in other words, land prices would fall if planning restrictions were lifted.[8] These kinds of arguments have long been propounded by neoclassical economists of a liberal persuasion, leading to suggestions that planning should take more of a backseat in housebuilding decisions or focus on actively channelling land to housebuilders.[9]

There are reasons, though, to suggest that this approach would not work. Landowners might be resistant to selling at lower prices than they expected their land to fetch, particularly as landownership is seen in many societies as a safe and appreciating investment. So removing planning 'restrictions' might not bring land prices down; landowners may just wait for the abolition of planning restrictions to be reversed or market pressures to push prices up again. Second, housebuilders themselves have some interest in keeping house prices high in general relative to the price at which they are able to negotiate land deals. This means that housebuilders are not interested in flooding the market with new housing to bring house prices down. Third, even with more land and more housebuilding, meeting market demand will satisfy the needs of only a section of the population – those that can afford market rents and prices. And fourth, it is important to recognise that the pressures for increasing the demand for housing (including the central importance of the availability of credit) may continue to have a significant impact on house prices and hence land prices.

Another problem with relying on the private sector to deliver the amount of housing needed is volatility in the housebuilding sector.

—

Private housebuilders are subject to the vagaries of market processes, making the delivery of a basic human need dependent on the ups and downs of the market place. The credit crunch of the first decade of the 21st century resulted in severe restrictions on credit in many countries, such as the UK and the US, affecting both developers wanting money to buy land and run their businesses and households needing mortgage loans to buy houses.[10] Combined with increased foreclosures in the housing market, the result was falling house prices and a lack of new building.

Finally, even if market processes could deliver all the housing that was needed, it would do so at a cost. This could be the loss of valued heritages, beloved landscapes and much-used open spaces. Planning is an activity that tries to balance the many, different impacts of new development. It seeks to make sure that new development meets the needs and expectations of local communities and sometimes these needs and expectations involve restrictions on development. We explore these aspects of planning further in Chapter Six.

So, if the level of new housebuilding cannot be left to the market, how can planning decide what the level of such development should be? Looking just at individual proposals for developing specific sites, one by one, leaves the issue of how much new housing is provided in an area to the fit between the sites that come forward from developers and the local assessment of individual sites. If local planning favours the conservation of local heritage and character, relatively little new housing might be provided. If it favours an ordinance for small housing units, there might be a rush for building such units leading to an excess of supply over demand due to the limited number of single-person households locally.

This throws the emphasis back onto the process by which the total amount of desired housebuilding in a locality is decided. In some societies this is a decision taken locally, in some regionally and in some nationally. The balance of political pressures at these different scales will of course determine to what extent meeting housing need is a priority and what the other priorities for planning in that area are. There is also the question of how far building new houses will contribute to meeting housing need in that locality and how well this relationship is understood. All these factors will drive the decisions about what the level of housebuilding should be.

In the UK the setting of housebuilding numbers to date has been a fairly centralised process. Central government saw new housebuilding as a key way of meeting housing need directly through providing homes and indirectly through driving down the overall level of house prices. This resulted in national housing targets. In 2007, the government announced a target of 3 million homes by 2020.[11] These targets were then cascaded down to the regional level, where they were enshrined in regional housing targets. And these, in turn, then influenced the land allocations and policies in the most local level of plans, in Local Development Plan Documents. However, whether the pattern of actual development matches these housing numbers depends on the development market and the decisions of housebuilders. In April 2010, the chairman of the National Housing Federation claimed that regional housing targets were not being met in any of the English regions.[12]

This could be used to used to argue for a less passive approach in relation to market processes of housebuilding. However, the new UK government elected in 2010 has instead decided to abolish national and regional housebuilding targets. It is leaving the decision on how many new houses should be built in an area to local authorities at the district and city level. Given the local political pressures that often exist against new development, this has raised considerable concern over the impact of the new approach on total housebuilding numbers. Localist planning is likely to be more effective in restricting development than national and regional targets were in promoting it. The government's proposal for small-scale rural development to be permitted outside the planning system if supported by a local referendum is unlikely to make a significant impact on overall numbers. It may, however, impact on local demand for facilities and there are, therefore, some concerns over the implied lack of integration with spatial planning at the scale beyond the village or hamlet.

But if a reliance on market-based developers puts the planning system in a rather passive position with regard to promoting housebuilding, rather more influence can be exercised as to the type of housing that is built. Whether through zoning ordinances, negotiation on specific development applications or building codes, it is widespread practice for the standard and specification of new dwellings to be strongly influenced, even mandated by the planning system. Safety standards of new build, space standards, design quality, energy efficiency and noise insulation have all been influenced in this way. Most recently there has been an emphasis on making new residential development more sustainable by requiring a range of features (discussed further in Chapter Seven).

However, the ability of a planning system to require changes to new development in line with specific requirements is going to depend on the costs of those changes and the profitability of development. Too many requirements and profit levels will fall, resulting in some developments being discouraged. Thus there may be a trade-off between reaching targets for a given quantity of new housing and attaining desired standards for each house built. In time, though, markets will adjust to these expected standards, internalising the costs (and eventually passing some of them to landowners in the form of lower land prices) and this trade-off will become less severe.

The location of housebuilding

Clearly the decisions about how much new housebuilding to have and where this housing should go are interrelated. If the consensus is that a substantial amount of building is needed in an area, then more and more sites will be considered for possible development. But what are the general principles by which sites are identified as desirable locations for development?

Many of the features of new housing that make it desirable relate to the details of the development: the layout of the estate, the design of the individual houses and the standard and type of construction method. However, there are features which depend on the location of the housing in relation the surrounding area, both the immediate locality and the broader settlement. These fall into three categories: the relationship to infrastructure of all kinds; the impact on overall patterns of urban form; and the question of what is being replaced.

As Chapter Two has already discussed, in modern societies we expect our homes to be connected to the various infrastructure networks that allow us to live as we would wish to. Given that we are rarely starting with a completely clean sheet on the drawing board in deciding the location of development, a central issue in allocating housebuilding sites is how they relate to the existing patterns of infrastructure. Planning on a regional and local scale often starts from a mapping of these infrastructures in deciding which sites to prioritise for development. Given that such infrastructures are costly to put into place, it makes sense to maximise their efficiency by placing new development where spare capacity in the networks can be used. This applies as much to water infrastructure as to school capacity.

Of course, as discussed in Chapter Two, these infrastructures could be expanded. New pipelines and sewers can be built; new schools and doctors' surgeries created. But this raises the issue of the costs of such expansion and who bears these costs. Where the private housebuilder bears the costs, this can act as an incentive for new development to be efficiently located. But it is often the case that the developer bears only part of the additional costs of providing these services and facilities. The public sector usually picks up a substantial part of the financial burden of infrastructure provision. Therefore, there is a financial imperative for the planning system to locate new development in a cost-effective way where infrastructure is concerned.

These kind of considerations have been part of the reason for promoting new settlements on a sufficient scale to meet housing need while ensuring the most efficient and cost-effective use of infrastructure. The British New Towns programme is an example of this kind of initiative.[13] In that programme mass housebuilding was planned around new infrastructure: new road networks, new water and sewer pipes, new schools and new hospitals. The watchwords of the programme were a rational use of land and resources to meet housing need.

For less comprehensively planned new development, a different approach is needed. In the US, impact fees are charged on new development to fund infrastructure requirements. As from April 2010, local authorities in England and Wales can operate a Community Infrastructure Levy, which builds closely on the spatial planning

—

approach. The idea is that the local authority will look at the amount of new development that is planned for their locality within their planning documents. They will also consider the planned level of investment in all the different kinds of infrastructure that are already in the pipeline of different public and private sector organisations. The gap between this and the demands generated by the new development will be assessed and the infrastructure required to fill this gap will be worked out. When costed, this will produce a bill for the 'gap' infrastructure and this can be divided by the planned new development to produce a levy on each dwelling or each square metre of commercial space. In this way the resources will be made available to ensure that new development will be adequately serviced with appropriate infrastructure.

Increasingly, though, planning is looking to broader resource-efficiency in considering the location of development vis-à-vis infrastructure. In the context of concerns about long-term sustainability, it is not just the financial cost of servicing new development that is important but also the demands that are put on environmental services such as water supply and climate protection. This encourages the planning system to locate developments where water and energy can be supplied sustainably over the long term. Within urban areas, the location of new development is being considered in relation to the overall heat load for district heating schemes and the capacity of decentralised energy systems. New developments are being seen in the context of the surrounding existing built environment in making such judgements, so that neighbourhood energy, heating and cooling requirements can be considered.

New settlements are again being promoted as a means of delivering resource efficiency, not just cost-efficiency. In the UK, eco-towns have been suggested as the most effective and efficient way of delivering energy-efficient homes by building to high efficiency standards but also connecting into innovative means of decentralised renewable energy generation at the scale of a new town.[14] (However, current public sector finance cuts may jeopardise the implementation of the eco-towns programme.) In China, the eco-city of Dongtan has been advertised in similar resource-efficiency terms.[15]

—

Sustainability concerns also inform the desire to influence the overall shape of urban areas, their urban form. The idea that towns and cities have an ideal shape is an old one. Many histories of urban planning start with pictures of settlements from Roman and European medieval times, when cities were bounded by their walls, largely for military purposes. They continue with images from the great 20th-century architects such as Le Corbusier and Lloyd Wright designing whole settlements from an aerial perspective in which the aesthetics of the overall pattern was a dominant concern.[16]

Aesthetics and strategic concerns continue to intermingle in decisions about urban form. In England, it has long been argued that planning seeks to contain urban areas.[17] There are multiple rationales for this: conserving agricultural land, promoting efficient urban development, protecting the countryside, and keeping individual urban areas distinct and separate from each other. The idea of the green belt, while it has roots going back to public health concerns in Tudor England, has been a key means of preventing development within an area girdling a city and thus shaping urban growth.[18] The strength of these concerns underpins planning for conservation, explored in Chapter Five.

More recently, this same agenda has been harnessed to the reduction of energy consumption in travel and the promotion of more energy-efficient settlements as a means of reducing carbon dioxide emissions. This has become a significant factor in debates on where new development should go. The core of the idea is that new development should avoid urban sprawl and should contribute to densifying urban areas, in other words, to increasing the overall urban density. This can be achieved in a number of ways (say, by zoning or negotiation), although the current coalition government in the UK has rejected the use of mandatory minimum densities for residential development.

It is argued that increased densities have the potential to reduce carbon emissions from car travel by reducing the distance driven, encouraging more walking and cycling and (provided that development is near to public transport stations and stops) greater use of public transport systems, making them more viable. This provides a strong basis for moving the location of new housebuilding away from

—

greenfield sites and instead looking for undeveloped or underused land within the urban envelope. In the UK, this has been achieved by encouraging new development on land defined as brownfield, that is, land previously developed with an urban use.

But deciding where new housebuilding should go inevitably involves deciding where it should not go. As the reference to urban containment makes clear, the desire to put more development within urban boundaries was also significantly a desire to avoid building on the countryside. Planning, even when considering new development proposals, is also about protecting existing urban and rural areas. Recently in the UK, the government has decided that too many large gardens have been used for housebuilding – so-called 'garden grabbing' – and therefore gardens have been removed from the definition of brownfield land. Thus considering what would be lost to a new housing development is an important dimension of planning the location of housebuilding.

Sieve analysis has become a traditional means of informing the location of new development, now often using geographic information systems. In such an analysis, areas where development should be resisted, say on the ground of landscape, heritage or nature conservation value, are mapped out and areas that fall between the mapped areas are identified as potential development sites. Concerns about the impacts of climate change mean that such analyses are now also considering the resilience of urban development and seeking to locate new housing in areas that it will not be at high risk of flooding from sea level rise or runoff during periods of heavy rainfall. In the UK, development in floodplains is increasingly restricted, so that they are available to absorb such runoff.

However, this discussion of how the location of development sites is planned should not ignore the significance of so-called 'windfall sites' to overall new housing numbers.[19] Allocations of housing land tend to focus on the larger sites, which can be readily identified as a distinct development opportunity. But there is a significant quantum of new housing that is provided by development on infill and backland sites and by conversions from other uses.

These include building on the small sites that are formed by the changing patterns of land use in urban areas: the garages behind

—

housing streets, ends of gardens and the odd-shaped parcels of land between other developments. The often contentious redevelopment of a large house and its garden for a block of flats falls into this category. And they also include the continuous process of adaptation that occurs within urban areas as floors above shops become more valuable as converted flats rather than storage areas, or small workshops become unprofitable and hence ripe for redevelopment. The aggregate implications of such development can be difficult to foresee or to control.

The implications for the planning system

So what does the previous discussion tell us about the implications for the planning system of the role of market processes in delivering new housing? It suggests that the housebuilding industry has a rather contradictory set of requirements. It would like planning to release land so that building can take place. It wants enough land allocated to reduce the power of landowners so that land can be purchased cheaply. But allowing too much housebuilding may drive house prices down and make it more difficult to sell new houses without undue delay. Housebuilders will have to resort to building out their sites more slowly in such circumstances, which is an expensive way to hold onto land.

Housebuilders will also want to avoid long delays in getting development permission. The speedier the process can be completed the better, from a developer's perspective. They will want to avoid wasting time on unsuccessful attempts to get development permission. They want a degree of certainty from the planning system so that they can judge more accurately the risk in getting permission on any particular site. However, they still want the opportunity to make a profit by obtaining development permission on an unexpected site. This involves housebuilders buying land without development permission or even any apparent prospect of development permission and then using their knowledge of the planning system to obtain such permission.

And when they get that development permission, they will want to avoid restrictions that reduce the profit of the development. This

—

means avoiding requirements for a more costly form of development unless this expenditure will be recovered by charging a premium price to housebuyers. It will mean trying to minimise the planning gain that a planning authority may try to extract on behalf of the local community. And it will mean trying to get as many units onto the site as needed to maximise the total development value of the site.

Eventually higher densities will drive the price of individual units down to a point where the total revenue from sales of all units falls. It may push a development from one market niche to another – from executive housing to middle-income housing. But generally, for a housebuilder, higher densities and more units means more development profit. So local planning can encourage development by allowing higher density development; where this is also seen to support urban regeneration and/or sustainability, then this is a happy coincidence.

Where most new housing results from market-led development, these requirements need to taken seriously in considering to what extent the planning system can meet housing need. A reliance on market processes to produce residential development, and therefore on engagement between planning processes and market actors, is part of the reason why the planning system is in an essentially passive role. But there are alternatives. The resources (financial and legislative) of government can be used to make planning for housebuilding more proactive.

As Chapter One suggested, in some countries at certain times national or local governments have intervened more proactively in land markets. They have built up land banks so that developers have to or can buy land directly from the planning body, allowing that body to exercise influence through its role as landowner. Alternatively, planning authorities have used their powers of purchasing land (compulsorily or voluntarily) to assemble sites for development and/or to divide it into appropriate land parcels. This provides much more direct potential for deciding where development should occur and even for influencing the type of houses built and the prices at which they are sold.

And, of course, in some countries and at certain times state-led housebuilding has been significant. In the UK, local authority-built

—

council housing constituted a significant proportion of new build up until the 1980s, when the right-to-buy policy was introduced.[20] Alternatively, the state can subsidise development by so-called third sector bodies such as housing associations, charities, and community organisations. In some European countries, the majority of housing is provided to rent through such means. This provides a different context for the planning system, with the possibility of much more influence over housebuilding patterns.

Planning and affordable housing

How can planning deliver affordable housing and, indeed, is this a task for which the planning system should have prime responsibility? We have seen that a planning system can be operated to reduce the price of houses by releasing a lot of land, although the extent of this fall depends on the willingness of landowners to sell their land and builders to keep building out those sites.

The impact of planned releases of land also depends on what is happening to the market for housing overall. House prices are the result of the interaction of demand and supply. New housebuilding is only a part of the overall supply of housing, with the majority of housing in most areas being made up from turnover in the existing stock. The willingness of existing owners to put their property onto the market and sell it at the price buyers want to pay will be a big influence on house prices. In market downturns, this aspect of supply often dries up and that can limit the fall in house prices.

And the demand side is a major influence on overall levels and changes in house prices. Few people can afford to buy their home outright; they usually depend on long-term credit in the form of a mortgage. The terms on which such credit is made available are centrally important in determining housing demand. When mortgages are readily available, the size of mortgages is high relative to household income and interest rates are low, then demand will be increased and this will push house prices up. Since these factors are tied up with national economic policy, there may be macroeconomic reasons for keeping credit easy and cheap and this will work against low house prices. In such circumstances, releasing land for housebuilding will generate profits for housebuilders but is unlikely to reduce house prices substantially, because of the pressure of credit-fuelled demand.

But this is only relevant where owner-occupation is the dominant housing tenure. In England, about 70% of households were in owner-occupation in 2007.[21] For such people their home is not only a place of shelter, safety and a means of expressing their identity, it is also an investment and a source of financial security (or loss). Not all countries have significant levels of owner-occupation and this makes a big difference to how housing is viewed.

In a country where owner-occupation is the norm, then lower prices may be beneficial for people trying to enter the housing market for the first time, but it represents a loss in the capital value of the most significant investment made by most households. Indeed many households enter the housing market in anticipation of this asset – their home – appreciating in value. They are understandably reluctant to see its value go down. In a country with high levels of renting in the housing sector, the demand for new development will come from potential landlords, the buy-to-let sector and housing institutions of different kinds. For this sector, falling development prices mean falling rents and this is to the benefit of households; it is the existing landlords who feel the pain.

But lower housing prices and rents are not the same as falling prices and rents. For low prices and rents (relative to household income) to become an established feature of housing markets, there would need to be adjustments in building and land markets. Technological change and economies of scale in building materials, components and methods might drive construction costs down, which could lead to low house prices becoming the norm. Alternatively, adjustments in the land market (due to taxation, regulation or legislation, for instance) could alter relationships between developers and landowners so that land prices fall to new lower levels and stay there. Indeed, without such measures to keep the price of residential development land at low levels, affordable private sector housing is unlikely to be achievable.

All of this reinforces the point that manipulating the planning system as a way of achieving affordable house prices is a difficult policy

—

to pursue successfully. It is an approach riven with contradictions, particularly in countries with high levels of owner-occupation and where housebuilders have looked to development gains for part of their profits. In any case, relying on the private sector will never meet the housing needs of all sectors of society in terms of providing an affordable, high-quality dwelling for all households.

To meet this social goal effectively, there needs to be investment in subsidised housing for rent through the public sector or the third sector. This is the remit of housing policy, not of the planning system, although innovative planning policies can encourage more social housing. This has been the case in England, where planning policies have required a percentage of houses built in a development to be affordable, that is, sold at lower prices to certain public sector workers, sold on a shared ownership basis or available to rent through a registered social landlord.[22] New government policies will seek to encourage the continued provision of affordable housing by giving local authorities an additional sum of money at least equivalent to the current property tax for each affordable house built.

However, the delivery of affordable housing depends not only on the allocation of sites but also on the subsidies to the providers of such housing. Thus partnership between planning and housing policy to provide adequate subsidy to the social housing sector seems the best way to ensure that everyone has their human right to adequate housing met.

FOUR

Downtown

Planning for new housebuilding is about how urban growth is managed, but another important aspect of planning is how it responds to urban decline. This chapter turns to concerns about urban poverty and the role of planning in urban regeneration. What causes urban decline? How has the planning system responded and what has been learnt from past mistakes? How are the private sector and local communities involved in planning for urban regeneration? What are the limitations to current models of such regeneration?

The roots of urban decline

Travelling across any city will reveal unevenness in the quality of life of residents and the level of local economic activity. Some areas will be buoyant, with thriving shops, high-value private property and a good standard of public space. Others will have vacant properties, derelict spaces and evidence of low incomes and high unemployment. Such unevenness seems to be an inherent feature of a market-based economy. Market processes sort land and local areas to create areas of high or low economic values. There are a number of reasons for this.

Partly, the spatial unevenness of economic activity is a reflection of the inequalities of income in society. However, land and property markets seem to encourage concentration of different income groups, creating distinct sub-markets at the scale of the urban neighbourhood so that people of a certain income level are more likely to be located near other households in a similar income band.[1] This can be accentuated by planning policies, such as zoning ordinances that require property of a certain size to be built in a given area, effectively setting a minimum property value on the houses there. Mortgage lending policies can also have an effect, as when more capital is loaned

—

in high value areas on the basis that they are less risky (there is less likelihood of property devaluation), thus keeping property values high in a self-fulfilling prophesy. School performance can have a similar effect. If there is a good local public sector school, then families who can afford it will pay more to move into the catchment area for the school, pushing up local property prices and creating a middle-class enclave around the high-performing school.[2] And finally, where local tax revenues depend on either the value of local sales or local property, then there will be more available in higher income areas for investment back into these areas.[3] These are all examples of how a high-value property area can be maintained by a virtual cycle of cause and effect.

By contrast there will be areas across cities that are locked-into a vicious cycle, whereby low local incomes reinforce low levels of economic activity and opportunity, low property prices, low tax revenue and low investment in the public realm. This economic segregation between different income groups can be reinforced by institutionalised racism in labour and property markets so that different ethnic groups are also separated and concentrated across the space of the city.[4]

These dynamics are complex, resulting from many different aspects of market and social processes. Nevertheless, urban planning has often been charged with tackling the 'urban' problem of economic and social disadvantage. Given its emphasis on land use, spatial organisation and urban development, planning systems have tended to do so by promoting particular forms of new development, that is, property-led urban regeneration. The logic is that encouraging, through various means, certain patterns of new development will attract economic investment into an area, providing jobs and lifting local incomes. The history of this approach suggests lessons for current urban regeneration practice.

Modernist urban regeneration

Planning's experience with urban regeneration has not been an entirely happy one. Some of the worst examples of planning practice are associated with the wholesale clearance and redevelopment of inner city areas that typified urban planning in the mid-20th century.[6] The desire to engage in such large-scale redevelopment in Britain and other European countries arose partly from the bomb damage experienced during World War Two. But clearance and redevelopment was also a feature of urban regeneration in other countries, locations and times, a way of responding to the poor living conditions of lower income groups in cities generally. Wholesale redevelopment was seen as a way of dealing with the social and economic condition of poverty by replacing the physical environment lived in by the poor.

There was a strong element of physical determinism in this thinking; in other words, the view that the poor would behave differently by living in a different physical environment and this would enable them to lift themselves out of conditions of poverty.[7] This idea of physical determinism is a thread running through much planning activity. The goals that planning systems are charged with can be very extensive and seem to be growing all the time. Yet the main lever that the planning system can use is influence over the physical environment. Thus, to support the idea that the planning system has a significant role to play in meeting societal goals, the assumption has to be made that changing the physical environment will lead to broader social and economic changes.

It is unquestionable that our physical environment does make a difference – to how we live, our behaviour and what we get out of life. The question is how much of a difference it makes and what else is required to achieve desired outcomes. Changing the built fabric is not always sufficient on its own. Unemployment, low income levels, antisocial behaviour and unsustainable lifestyles can be influenced by physical change in the built environment but complementary policies will also be required. Economic development needs more than new factories and workspaces; poverty reduction needs more than better housing; antisocial behaviour will not respond simply to improved public spaces; and sustainability is a matter of changed behaviour on energy consumption, waste recycling and so on, which only partly results from energy-efficient built stock and recycling facilities.

The idea that urban life could be made better by physical change in the urban environment has been compounded in the past by the modernist approach to the planning itself. As applied to urban regeneration, this model sees the planning organisation acting as the developer or, at least, as the leader of the redevelopment process. The financial resources come from within the public sector, so that the constraints of raising market finance are not as significant. Rather, the commercial sector is providing a service to the public sector, which has the power of being the fee-paying client. It is the public sector that is in control.

The outcomes of such modernist urban regeneration have often proved to be highly unsatisfactory. Many of the resulting urban redevelopments were seen, in retrospect, to be deeply flawed, unloved by local communities and dysfunctional in terms of creating prosperous and safe areas. This was compounded by a particular architectural aesthetic associated with modernism, which is often described as brutalist. Suffice it to say that this aesthetic, as put into practice by cash-limited public authorities, did not provide high-quality urban environments in many cases.

A particular criticism laid at the door of such urban regeneration was that local communities were largely ignored within the modernist approach. There tended to be only limited consultation of the local residents, with the assumption that the planners were better placed to make the key decisions. So perhaps it was not surprising that the resulting developments often did not meet the needs of their residents.

It was not just that the views of residents were ignored; there was insufficient attention to the dynamics within a local community that made an area function socially. These dynamics are related to the physical layout and construction of an area but cannot be reduced to these physical elements. They involve the relationships between people in a locality and the way that they constitute a community. The emphasis on physical redevelopment, the assumption of physical determinism shaping the behaviour of local communities and a lack of attention to these social dynamics within existing communities all contrived to produce the break-up of many existing communities during the redevelopment process.[8]

Urban regeneration and urban communities

The emphasis on public sector-led modernist planning of urban areas through their physical redevelopment has yielded a number of key lessons and these have shaped more recent urban regeneration practice, leading to a stronger emphasis on urban design and community engagement within a property-led approach.

First, it became clear that this approach to urban redevelopment was lacking an understanding of the social dynamics within existing urban communities.[9] In particular, the social capital that is built up within such a local community was being ignored. Social capital is an essential element of the functioning of a community. Defined as close networks of links between people, combined with common norms of trust, reciprocity and mutuality, social capital is what turns a collection of people into a community. In a community, people not only know each other but trust each other, rely on each other and do favours for each other in the knowledge that this benefits everyone.

What many modernist redevelopments did was to destroy the networks that constitute social capital along with the existing physical environment. It proved much more difficult to recreate such capital and therefore the local community was also effectively destroyed. This kind of destruction occurred even when a community, usually a working-class community, was re-housed together in a new development. The social capital did not survive the physical transplantation. This was a lesson that was painfully learned and attempts to avoid such destruction were made in postmodernist urban regeneration, by handling demolition plans much more sensitively and investing in keeping community structures alive and operational during the regeneration process.

Another form of community destruction occurred when redevelopment and refurbishment of an area resulted in the local community – a low-income community – being displaced by incoming higher-income groups, attracted by the improving environment and the investment gains of buying cheap property in anticipation of rising property values. Gentrification, as this process is known, largely arises from the market dynamics concerning owner-occupied properties within regeneration areas.[10] A degree of

—

gentrification is usually regarded as a sign of success in regeneration projects. Attracting a wider range of social groups into living in the area is evidence of the area becoming more buoyant.

However, to avoid displacement of the very community that the regeneration project is intended to benefit requires careful consideration of different housing tenures across the project. The aim is a mix of tenures and, with that, a mix of social groups. The policy of requiring a percentage of every private sector residential development to comprise affordable housing (mentioned in Chapter Three) was usually fulfilled by involving a housing association (or registered social landlord) and offering this housing on a rental or shared ownership basis. Provided both the affordable and market housing is accommodated on the same or adjoining sites, then this policy results in a finer mixing of social groups and avoids both middle-class gentrification and working-class ghettoisation.

One way of ensuring that existing communities are not adversely affected by a regeneration project is to make sure that they, or rather representatives of local communities, are involved in the regeneration process.[11] This means making space within the organisational structures delivering regeneration for such community representatives to have a say. This can be quite onerous in terms of time and planning staff resources. For, while a grouping of residents may be termed a 'community', in reality they are likely to have many different needs and interests. Meeting the needs of the 'community' may include attention to the requirements of the elderly alongside young adults, active young children alongside the less physically able, different religious groups, different ethnic groups, the specific needs of women, and so on.

Whether the regeneration process opts for a single community organisation, which will hopefully internalise discussions over conflicts and different needs, or a mass of different modes of representation, the handling of community within regeneration efforts is likely to be a major task and involve considerable resources.

In addition to giving the local community a say in the regeneration effort, community engagement is likely to involve a degree of expectations management. For, as the next section will discuss, postmodernist urban regeneration is not driven by the availability of

—

public sector resources and the powers of the public sector. Rather, there is a recognition that the public sector can only leverage in private sector resources and that any regeneration depends on the continued interest of the private sector in the area. Encouraging the involvement of local communities within the regeneration process has to balance the raising of hopes as to how regeneration can meet the diverse needs of local communities, with some reality checking linked to the limitations of what commercially based development can and will deliver.

Urban regeneration and the private sector

In addition to the need to engage with local communities, modernist urban regeneration made it clear that a different kind of involvement of the private sector was necessary. This was partly as a result of the constraints on public sector budgets which started to bite after the world recession of the 1970s but also because it was recognised that one of the limitations of modernist planning was its weak understanding of market processes. Simply building new physical stock was insufficient; regeneration needed to build a new local economy. This puts the emphasis on the involvement of market actors, not just as contractors on a public sector-led project but as active participants in, and even directors of, the urban regeneration effort. The failures of modernist urban regeneration have led to an approach which cedes some of the planner's power to other actors, an approach fitting with the paradigm of governance.

Commonly termed a partnership approach, this involves a shift from what the public sector can do alone and a move instead to the benefits of bringing together all the actors who could contribute to the goal of regeneration.[12] The essence of a partnership approach is the recognition that the state on its own – in this case the planners and their public sector colleagues – does not have the capacity to fulfil the goals that have been set for it. So a partnership has to be built with actors from the different sectors: the different parts of the public sector, the commercial sector and the community sector.

The public sector is still a key partner (or perhaps this should read 'partners') within such a partnership. Part of the difficulty that

—

modernist planning faced was the inability to coordinate all the different elements within the public sector whose involvement was necessary for effective regeneration. With the growth of the public sector, these different sectors multiplied: transport, public estates, health, education, social services, community services, waste management, nature conservation, and so on.

In addition, in the UK, as in some other countries during the latter part of the 20th century, many of these roles were moved at least partially outside the public sector and certainly outside of local government. Local planning authorities had to work with other public sector organisations and agencies and with private sector bodies fulfilling some of these functions. Networking with such bodies and steering them towards meeting urban regeneration goals became necessary.

Private sector bodies also became increasingly important within such networking. Quite apart from any public sector functions that were moving into the private sector, it became recognised that private sector bodies had to be major players within urban regeneration. While public sector housing could be built using a model in which the state paid the construction industry for a product and acted as a client, broader urban regeneration required a range of land uses and associated economic activities. And this meant involving the private sector in a different way, as a partner in development not as the supplier.

Since it was recognised that the private sector would not get involved in the areas requiring regeneration without the involvement of the public sector as well, the dominant mode of planning became leverage planning.[13] In this approach a certain quantum of public sector monies is used to underpin development of the area and attract in private sector monies. The aim is to achieve as high a leverage ratio as possible: four times as much private sector investment as the original public sector funding is preferable to only twice as much. Such an approach was lauded as not only more effective in delivering urban regeneration but also more efficient in terms of how public monies were spent.

The role of public sector planners is, therefore, to tackle all the barriers that currently exist to such profitable, higher-value

—

development. This may involve new planning policies or zoning for land, subsidies or compulsory purchase to overcome the overvaluation of land, site assembly from fragmented parcels to create viable development sites, and remediation of contaminated land. In short, the resources of the government can be brought into the regeneration scheme to overcome the key problems that face private sector developers and inhibit profitable development.

The problem with leverage planning is that the aim of driving up leverage ratios can mean that the private sector achieves a dominant say in what the area should look like and unprofitable land uses, such as housing for low-income households and community facilities, become marginalised. Where the aim is to redevelop an area primarily for commercial activities, as with a shopping centre or industrial park, it may be argued that this is not such a problem. However, this raises the question of why public funds or other resources are needed at all to support development that is essential commercial. Where the aim is a broader form of urban regeneration meeting the needs of inner-city communities, who are usually multiply disadvantaged, then too large a say for the private sector may undermine the whole purpose of the regeneration effort.

The skill of planning in the context of leverage-based regeneration is to use public sector funding for the scheme to attract private sector finance and then to ensure that the overall plan for the area meets a mix of social needs, including both profitable and unprofitable land uses, rather that just pump-priming private profit. Central to this approach will be the negotiation of so-called planning gain, whereby some of the financial benefits of the development are directed towards meeting particular local community needs, say a nursery or a local park.

Regulation is a potentially powerful lever within planning processes. The control it gives planners over the development process offers the scope for planning gain to deliver social benefits from new development for the local community. In the UK, some local authorities operate a systematic tariff system to ensure that part of the profits of development support infrastructure improvements. In Milton Keynes, an agreement was reached between the local council and the main housebuilders involved in the extension of the town on the portfolio of new infrastructure that would be required. This was costed and, when divided by the planned amount of new development, resulted in an infrastructure tariff of £18,500 for each new house and about £67 per square metre of commercial floorspace.[14]

In the London Borough of Southwark, the council has an online tool that works out the impacts of a proposed new development on local social and environmental infrastructure.[15] Again, these impacts are costed and a total amount for providing the infrastructure is then generated. For the flatted development currently being built in northern Southwark, this amounts to about £6,000 per flat. As in Milton Keynes, this sum becomes the subject of a legal agreement, known as a Section 106 agreement, to be signed by the local authority and the developer, committing the developer to paying this sum before the development can go ahead. As discussed in Chapter Two, this has now been generalised into the Community Infrastructure Levy.

The aim is that at the end of the regeneration effort the area will comprise a new mix of land uses and developments that combine market viability with social needs. What such regeneration efforts are less able to control is the effect of successful regeneration on local property markets. Insofar as profitable commercial activities are part of the regeneration scheme, then increased profitability will drive up commercial property values. As the area becomes more viable, vibrant and attractive, this is likely to drive up private housing rents and prices also. Planners often find themselves in a Catch 22 with such leverage regeneration, since bringing the area within the compass of buoyant property markets is both the aim of regeneration and also potentially threatens to turn such regeneration simply into commercial development with limited social side-benefits. For example, if the strategy is to take a low-income and low-value inner city area and incorporate it into the more buoyant central business district property market, then the area will change considerably in a way that the local community may not entirely welcome.

These concerns over how leverage-based regeneration may impact on the needs of disadvantaged groups has led to a third approach to regeneration, based on bottom-up community activism. This approach also needs a degree of public sector support, direction and coordination, but the focus of the public sector is primarily on the community and not on the private sector. In this approach, the community is enabled, indeed empowered, to meets its own needs, rather than relying on the side-effects of commercial development.

This form of regeneration has much in common with community-based initiatives in lower income countries.[16] The kinds of activity encompass time banks (in which members of a community exchange services that they can offer, say childcare for gardening), community gardens (which can support healthy eating campaigns as well as offering cheap food) and micro-credit schemes (in which small amounts of money are loaned to people considered bad credit risks by banks in order to set up small businesses or manage family finances).

In these schemes there is a focus on using the resources of local people, resources which are undervalued in a market system. Unemployed people still have skills, even if they cannot find payment for them in the labour market; they are uncommercial skills, yet often vital ones such as childcare and DIY that keep households going. By operating outside of market processes, these initiatives can enable the resources of such people to be released. The emphasis is on people exchanging skills to produce goods and services of value to each other. They are often not traded for money, or, if they are, tend to be offered within the local community at low prices. There is the prospect that this might lead to business activity that offers goods and services on the wider market but this is not the primary purpose.

Community or not-for-profit shops can also play a role here, providing a service at low cost, some employment opportunities and an outlet for local horticultural produce and locally made products. In addition such shops can be a social focal point and meeting place. In Blockley, in the Cotswolds, the community shop also houses a post office, a café, a nursery and community noticeboard and is a hub of village life. Its presence differentiates Blockley from many of the surrounding dormitory villages.

There is an argument that such community-based action is much better placed to deliver truly sustainable outcomes with environmental as well as social benefits.[17] This is particularly the case where the local community is using or managing local environmental

—

resources, such as a local river that could also provide fish, or local allotments that could provide fruit, vegetables and eggs, and not-for-profit shops and community centres. Here there is a strong synergy between sustainable use of that water- or land-based resource and the contribution to meeting social needs. This argument can be extended to cases where the community uses its own labour and ideas to promote innovative waste management, building insulation and energy generation schemes. Here the local community can be made more resilient at the same time as contributing to wider environmental goals.

However, important as such community building can be, it remains the exception rather than the rule. Regeneration activities continue to be focused around the role of the private sector and driven by market dynamics indicating what the desirable form and content of change should be. It is only in areas that have been abandoned by market actors that a reliance on such grass-roots regeneration emerges. Indeed it often needs the absence of attention by the private sector to provide a space within which community activities can flourish. Once the market identifies an area as potentially valuable, this can readily drive out community regeneration.

The revival of the case for demolition

In the immediate aftermath of the failures of modernist redevelopment being revealed, there was a backlash against demolition of existing buildings, particularly housing, to make way for new development. There was instead a growth of interest in refurbishment on a building by building basis, sometimes within the framework of area improvement schemes that amplified the benefits of individual refurbishment activities. Combined with the impact of conservation policies (discussed in Chapter Five), demolition rates of housing in the UK have fallen to very low levels of around 17,000 each year.[18]

But while the days of modernist regeneration, in which large areas of housing are demolished to make way for grand redevelopment schemes, may seem to be in the past, demolition has continued to play a role in regeneration, particularly where mixed land uses are concerned. Demolition can also be combined with the retention of

—

iconic buildings and some local refurbishment. Even demolition of large housing areas is now again being considered a desirable option. Arguments have been put forward for demolition-based regeneration on economic, social and environmental grounds.

The economic argument is based on the view that an existing area has a very low market value. Indeed, buildings and sites may have a negative value, where all the costs of redevelopment outstrip the end value of a new building within current market conditions. In essence, the broader local environment is acting as a constraint on the potential for redeveloping individual sites and refurbishing the rest. The layout and form of the area, as well as the land use mix, requires change for its economic potential, as measured by property values, to be realised. The road layout is often taken as the starting point for redesigning such an area, together with reconsidering the massing of the buildings. Thereafter urban design can create a higher-value environment.

Here the role of planning is to promote a masterplan for the area that will maximise its economic value, paying careful attention to how the pattern of land uses enhances the overall value of the area by each use complementing its neighbours. The layout of streets and public spaces should maximise flows of people where needed for public safety, social conviviality and economic trade. Other areas should be designed for fostering a sense of local community among a group of residents. In all, the area should approximate to what is considered desirable among property seekers, boosting demand for property and hence property values.

This is the argument behind the Housing Market Renewal Programme in the UK. Under this scheme 12 areas in the North and Midlands have been identified as suffering from chronic low demand, which is driving down local housing conditions. Pathfinder partnerships have been set up in these areas comprising local authorities and other regional and local stakeholders:

> Pathfinders are working to ensure that people have a real choice about staying in their areas and are not forced out because of the poor quality of housing. They do this by providing a choice of better quality homes, through a

—

mix of refurbishment, clearance and replacement, as well as some environmental works. This complements the wide range of regeneration activity that is happening in many of these areas.[19]

The Pathfinders guide a programme of clearance and redevelopment together with new infrastructure investment (although there have been recent budget cuts to this programme). There is an emphasis on working at a sufficient scale to deliver regeneration and this necessarily implies selective demolition.

A social argument can also be made for large-scale demolition of the area where that is the wish of the residents themselves. Some housing areas, mainly but not only those in public ownership and management, are of such a low standard of maintenance and construction and so dysfunctional in design that residents would welcome the disruption of demolition and redevelopment in order to obtain a new living environment. The difference between current and past approaches to such demolition is that the residents (hopefully) are kept fully involved in the decisions about demolition and the planning of the new area. In this way, demolition can fit into the partnership model of urban regeneration.

An example of this is provided by the Aylesbury Estate in south London. This is an area of about 28.5 hectares developed from 1963 to 1977 with a mix of housing including several large slab and high-rise blocks of flats with walkways. In total the area comprises 2,700 homes. Over 7,500 people are resident on the estate, overwhelmingly (83%) in local authority-owned accommodation. A total of 68% of the local community are from black and ethnic minority groups and 26 different languages are spoken in addition to English. The estate is in the third most deprived ward in the London Borough of Southwark, which itself is the eighth most deprived borough in England. However, the picture is not completely bleak. The level of educational attainment at GCSE (about 16 years old) is almost at the national average, having risen dramatically in the last decade and Aylesbury Estate children perform better than children elsewhere in the borough. Fear of crime has fallen and crime rates are below the borough average. Nevertheless there is evidence of social

—

deprivation and high unemployment, and the physical environment is of extremely poor quality.

The response to the problems on the estate has been to establish a New Deal for Communities (NDC) programme, spending some £56 million on social projects since 1999. In addition, in 2005, the decision was taken to demolish the estate and redevelop the site. Under an Area Action Plan, demolition is to proceed in stages over 15-20 years. The new development will be denser, providing 4,200 homes. Of these 2,100 will be 'affordable', mainly for rent but with about 500 available under shared ownership schemes. This means that there will be 2,100 homes built for sale, providing an income stream into the development. This will help fund the improved public spaces, community facilities and transport infrastructure for the estate.

The key to gaining acceptance of a plan largely based on demolition was engagement with the local community. As a result, at the public inquiry into the plans for the area, the local community appeared in support of the demolish-and-redevelop scheme. The NDC programme laid the groundwork for this. It claims that it has doubled the number of residents involved in local and voluntary organisations.[20] Three community resource centres have been provided and are well used; the NDC states that over 5,000 people per year use such facilities. The NDC has also supported over 68 projects for the local community and in 2008 43% of residents felt part of the local community. The social capital built up within the Aylesbury Estate community has supported plans for demolition and will hopefully maintain the community ties during the disruption of development, rehousing and demolition.

Finally, there has been a case put forward for increasing rates of demolition from an environmental sustainability perspective. The argument here is based on the difference between the energy efficiency standards of the current housing stock and that of state-of-the-art new build. While new housing has energy embodied in its materials and construction process, this can be quite rapidly offset by increased energy savings in a new house arising from lower requirements for space and water heating. In energy, and hence carbon, terms, the payback time for investing in new energy-efficient housing is relatively low.

—

The *40% House* analysis was undertaken by the Oxford University Environmental Change Unit[21] to assess how the housing sector could achieve a 60% reduction in carbon emissions by 2050. Building a new home to a high standard of energy efficiency is assumed to involve 90,000 kWh of embodied energy, while reducing annual energy consumption for space heating to 8,200 kWh per annum. This provides an energy payback period of about 13 years, so well before 2050. However, Boardman et al assume that new build could achieve higher standards of 2,000 kWh per annum, while refurbishment would only drive energy demand down to 9,000 kWh per annum. On this basis, they argue that there is a need to demolish 3.2 million properties between 2005 and 2050, or 80,000 dwellings per annum by 2016. They argue that demolition should focus on the worst 14% of the stock, in other words, a targeted demolition strategy.

This view has been criticised on a number of grounds.[22] First, the above conclusions are based on complex modelling and as such are highly dependent on the initial assumptions. Second, there is the possibility that refurbishment of existing housing can also achieve efficiencies that meet or even surpass those of standard new housing. The German Zukunft Haus programme is cited as evidence of this, achieving an 80% reduction in energy use. And third, there are the other costs of demolition programmes and redevelopment programmes: landfill disposal of waste materials; transportation of building materials; the rendering obsolete of existing infrastructure; and social disruption. Anne Power thus argues 'the overall balance of evidence suggests that refurbishment most often makes sense on the basis of time, cost, community impact, prevention of sprawl, reuse of buildings in both the short and long term'.[23]

The difficulty is that clearance and redevelopment seems a simpler policy to pursue than encouraging very large numbers of householders and landlords to undertake investments in their individual homes. These issues will be returned to in Chapter Six, focusing on the individual householder.

FIVE

This green and pleasant land

We have seen how development is driven by the mix of market pressures and public policy in the case of both new housebuilding and urban redevelopment. While the discussion of regenerating urban areas suggested a consensus about the benefit of new development, it did highlight the potential for resistance to demolition of existing residential areas. The account of planning for residential development also suggested potential resistance here. Why do people resist change? How is this related to the value that they place on existing and historic areas and buildings? How does this connect to the economics of land and property markets? And, moreover, what about the countryside and biodiversity, our natural heritage?

The desirability of conservation

Conserving valued aspects of towns, cities and the countryside is highly popular, particularly in developed countries. This can cover conservation of historic buildings, open spaces, specific trees, rare habitats, facilities used by local communities and even familiar street layouts, protecting them from the effects of new development. Membership of organisations that promote or undertake such conservation (such as, in the UK, the Civic Trust, English Heritage, Historic Scotland and the National Trust) is substantial. It has been reported that 1.5% of the UK population are paid-up environmental group members; that is about 1 million people. In the US the figure is as high at 15.6% and in the Netherlands an amazing 43.5%.[1] Proposals to demolish local landmarks can often result in vocal opposition and opinion polls record high support for conservation of heritage.

Why should this be the case? There are a number of different reasons that can be suggested. All of them emphasise the importance

---

of people's surroundings to how they feel about themselves. People often identify strongly with their local area, where they live. This is particularly the case when they have lived in the area a long time, possibly having been born and brought up there. But incomers to an area can also be vocal spokespersons for local areas; key features of the area may be the reason that they moved there and they are loath to see them disappear.

Such features of an area become part of people's everyday lives and it is difficult to imagine living without them. This can apply to all sorts of aspects of a locality: a church, market-place, post office, shop, swimming pool or open space. They are tied up with the relationships that people have with each other in the locality and with the sense of community. These are often places where people meet each other; if these places disappear then one set of contacts between people also disappears. And more than that, these features become closely associated with the identity of individuals, with their sense of self. When they are threatened, then all these aspects of social life are also threatened: sense of the locality, of the community and of self.

More generally, removing or even changing parts of the local environment, whether built or natural, challenges ideas of continuity and stability. The physical environment is usually one of the more enduring aspects of our lives. Even with redevelopment and refurbishment, it is only a relatively small percentage of the overall built stock that changes in any year. Between 1900 and 1998, the housing stock increased by less that 1% per annum.[2] Landscapes tend to outlive generations, barring large-scale primary resource exploitation and radical changes in agricultural or forestry practices. If these environments can change, then this is symbolic of change more generally.

Of course, not all countries find such change threatening or undesirable. This negative view of new development need not apply in all circumstances. Such development can be viewed positively, as enhancing the prosperity of an area. More households can mean more people buying goods and services in the local area, boosting the local economy and leading to a more buoyant town centre. More shops, offices and industry will mean more economic activity in a locality and more jobs. In more economically depressed areas, new development is usually positively encouraged by local communities to reverse the loss of local facilities. But in many relatively well-off areas, local communities often want to keep the area unchanged, to keep the existing way of life even if this means turning away the opportunity for local economic development.

This is one example of the way that planning debates key into deeply held cultural values about what constitutes the good life, how people want to live and how they view other groups within society. Although this tendency will clearly vary from country to country, there does seem to be a common theme of nostalgia for the period before industrialisation and urbanisation, which is clearly connected to the resistance to more urban development.

In the UK this is reflected in a vision of rural life which probably never existed but is nevertheless powerful as a cultural force.[3] It invokes the idea of a tightly knit local community, agriculture as a form of stewardship of the land and an acceptance of stable if hierarchical social relations. These cultural myths may seem a long way away from the mundane business of development, but they are powerful currents in society and inform the debates about where and how much development there should be. They are part of the reason why such debates are so emotive and cannot just be seen in terms of economic gain and loss.

It tends to be the higher-income countries that look back with nostalgia on their undeveloped environments. Other countries can see wholesale change in built and natural environments as a sign of progress. In China in the 21st century, the rate of development is seen as part of the country's economic progress and growing global profile. In postwar 20th-century Europe and the US, there was a similar pride in development as ushering in a new and better way of life while existing urban and rural environments were seen as old-fashioned and outmoded.

This association of physical change in environments with progress was part and parcel of modernism, which embraced technological change as advancement and saw the future as something to be rushed towards. This is another side to the modernist planning discussed in Chapters Two and Four as shaping the processes of strategic planning and urban regeneration. The attitude to change, a particular

—

aesthetics and a view of the power of planning are all wrapped up in such modernism. Furthermore, it is the disillusionment with many modernist planning initiatives of the 20th century that has led to a renewed interest in conservation and a questioning of the pace of urban redevelopment. This is not just born out of nostalgia for the past but also from actual experience of what can be lost when development happens too rapidly or carelessly.

Of course, not everyone within a society agrees on what to conserve and what to value. In deciding what to protect, there is an implicit judgement about whose views to take into account. Often what is involved is the different stake in the local area that different people have. Taking the opposition to new housebuilding as an example, the existing community have quite a different stake in the local area to the people who will buy the new housing and who may well come from outside the local area. Those buying the properties represent housing demand. If they are happy to buy the new housing at the going price then, by definition, they are happy with the quality of development and of the local environment; or, at least, they recognise that this is what they can get for the price they can afford.

Existing communities are judging the new developments on quite a different basis. They will be looking at the existing amenities, economic value and way of life associated with the existing area. The new housing may well change this for the worse. Land which was a green amenity will now be a housing estate. This loss of amenity may cause a loss in value for some property owners, as a pleasant view generally increases property prices. This may compound a general downward pressure or at least a lessening of the upward pressure on local house prices resulting from an increased supply of housing. Alternatively, the new housing may only be developed at prices that are out of reach for local people, particularly young couples. The new development for more affluent incomers may then create a high-priced housing market that forces local people to move away.[4]

And with the new housing come new households using the local area. This may mean more cars on the roads, more children wanting school places, more people queuing at the doctor's surgery. While incomers may put pressure on scarce social resources, they may work, shop and play outside the locality so that the potential for greater economic development in the locality is not realised.

There are also issues of change in the social mix of an area which may be resisted. Residents of higher-income areas may object to lower-priced housing, but equally lower-income households may fear the impact of higher-priced housing on the local housing market. Gentrification may be presented as a way of upgrading an area through new build and refurbishment, but the reality can be the replacement of existing working-class social groups with middle-class residents. Changes in social mix are changes to the communities that people are used to living within. A mixed community in which different social groups coexist and interact may be considered desirable from the point of view of society as a whole, but, in an already socially stratified world, creating such mixed communities can face resistance. So attitudes to conserving existing patterns of urban development are also about local people's attitudes to other social groups, of a different income level, a different background and from different areas.

Similar dilemmas are involved in considering how whole town centres may change, with one type of shop or outlet being replaced by another. There has been a vigorous debate about multiples (shops from established chains) replacing local shops and creating what has been termed 'clone town' in place of local distinctiveness.[5] Of course independent retailers take a wide range of forms; they may provide good local value for communities and keep a larger proportion of the money spent in shops within the local economy. But they may also represent higher-value sales and an absence of discount outlets that could provide a larger household basket for a given expenditure. One person's conservation of the status quo may be another's lost opportunity for improvement of their life chances.

In addition to the essentially political choices to be made about different people's views of what to conserve and when to allow development, there are judgements to be made about the balance between expert and community views. In some cases, these may coincide. Eminent historians and local conservation groups may agree that an Elizabethan manor house is an important historical building and it may be equally loved by local residents for the way

—

it contributes to the local setting. But in some cases local residents want to conserve a building that is not considered particularly rare or significant by expert opinion, and, in other cases local opinion will favour redevelopment of a building that experts consider to have historic value. The same kind of differences of opinion can result in locals valuing a scientifically unexceptional open space or dismissing the value of a rare natural habitat.

Expert opinion on conservation claims to speak for the collective judgement about what are important features in an area. It identifies elements of our joint built and natural heritage that are so important at a national or even global scale that their protection should be a high priority.[6] For example, the UK has 28 UNESCO recognised World Heritage Sites and 168 Ramsar sites (wetlands of international significance) covering over 1.25 million hectares. Turning to nature conservation areas of European significance (the Natura 2000 sites), there are 608 designated Special Areas of Conservation in the UK covering over 2.5 million hectares and 257 Special Protection Areas covering over 1.5 million hectares. In terms of the built environment, there are about 374,000 listed building entries for England and 9,300 Conservation Area designations (these are discussed further later in this chapter).

However, it is becoming recognised that established expertise about ecological, historical or anthropological value can learn from local communities and that local communities can offer a new perspective on what should be conserved. These local inputs may also be a form of expertise: local history societies have a wealth of knowledge of their area, as also do local wildlife groups. But there is also value in the non-expert opinions of local communities. This will bring multiple perspectives about conservation into planning.

These different views of what it is important to protect and conserve for future generations rest on different stories about people's past and about what defines the community and the place. In England, the experience of being the first industrial nation led to changes in attitude to the countryside. Rather than being a place of poverty and danger, it became seen as a place of peace and health, tamed through cultivation and landscaping. The great historic houses, castles and other buildings stand in this landscape as a specific narrative account

—

of England's long history. And the villages within this countryside become emblems of how this history can interleave with everyday life, offering a vision of living within a closely-knit community and in thatched, beamed and local stone cottages.

A quite different tale would be told of Scottish and Welsh heritage, reflecting national identities forged in opposition to the dominant English power.[7] In Scotland, the landscape offers a tale of battlefields and a land divided up among the English aristocracy with sheep and game replacing a peasantry forced into famine and exile. In Wales, the industrial heritage of mining (coal, slate and gold) creates the potential for a quite a different story of what the past was and what counts as worthy of preservation. And these are but a few examples of the many tales that could be told to justify the conservation of land and buildings and, with them, identity and history.

Increasingly, subaltern tales are being told, resurrecting the forgotten histories and heritage of, say, the working class or black Britains.[8] There is a growing acceptance that buildings and sites of importance from the point of view of working class and ethnic minority history are as important as the history of social elites. So multiple tales can be told of the history of a country and a local area, tales of the more or less powerful that would justify conservation efforts. In some countries the heritage of indigenous peoples is receiving particular attention in terms of celebrating their heritages: the Maori in New Zealand, the Aboriginal peoples in Australia, the Native Americans in North America and so on.[9] This movement is identifying new kinds of heritage sites that may not have been protected in the past. And this focus will increasingly shape the environment that is being saved for future generations enabling them to understand and appreciate their history, as well as creating places with meaning for current generations.

The kind of heritage that is conserved for the future and the balance between expert and lay views depends heavily on whose voice is given expression in debates about planning for conservation. Traditionally, it can be argued, middle-class and higher-income groups have had more of a say in which aspects of the built and natural environment should be protected from development.[10] This reflects the membership of many conservation bodies and the values that they espouse. Giving

—

a greater say to other groups within communities (for example, to working-class groups, younger people and ethnic minorities) will change the focus of conservation planning and, as a result, will shape future natural and built environments.

Conserving our built heritage

Conserving buildings is about much more than just preserving the physical fabric. It is about creating places that have meaning in all sorts of ways. So what is the role of planning in achieving this and how can it achieve it?[11]

A starting point is an understanding of which aspects of our built environment have sufficient value to conserve. Here planning can play a role in collecting and providing information. Age may be a visible feature of a building, but heritage value is not. Assessing this requires finding out about the past of a building within the locality and considering the significance of this past. Historical research based on written and drawn records is an important part of this assessment.

Moreover, as the previous discussion emphasised, expert assessment is only part of the process of determining if a building has heritage value. The views of the local community are also important, not only any oral history about the building and its use that can be gleaned from long-lived residents but also opinion on the value of the building to the area and its inhabitants today. So this is more than just information gathering. Planners are here engaging in a process of actively creating the category of a historic building, together with local communities and urban historians.

But urban heritage is more than just buildings, and historic buildings are valued more when they are in an appropriate setting. Thinking about the cultural and historic value of urban localities involves more than assessing individual buildings. Rather, the way that buildings relate to each other visually creates a village-, town- or cityscape and this contributes to the amenity, even beauty of the area. While not all old street plans and layouts are attractive, there is often something visually pleasing in developments that have grown organically over time, accruing bit by bit. Therefore planning has to understand how older buildings contribute to this local character, bringing design skills to bear in analysing the important features of both older and newer buildings and how they relate to each other in creating the experience of the urban environment.

Visual appeal is not the only significant criteria by which to judge older or mixed age areas, however. Such areas are not there primarily to be looked at but rather places where people come and go for work, leisure and family activities. Historic buildings often create areas that people are particularly attracted to for such activities. This involves understanding how such places function and what makes them work successfully as living environments. This is not a well understood field.[12] A backwater of jumbled streets can be a delightful spot to explore and become a focal point for interesting small shops, or it can be a deserted and therefore unappealing set of alleys that people won't venture into, with boarded-up buildings.

Historic buildings and areas are no guarantee of social vitality and economic vibrancy even if the physical fabric is valued by community and experts alike. Planning has a key task in working out how to make these more historic neighbourhoods function effectively within a modern village, town or city. This is where urban heritage interfaces with economic development, because the ready way to attract economic development is to allow physical development. Yet this very physical development can threaten the existing urban heritage.

It is usually considered cheaper to clear an area and build from scratch, particularly if the existing complex pattern of streets and buildings would curtail a layout that maximises lettable and sellable floorspace. Refurbishment of existing buildings can be costly compared with new build and this escalates if historic features need to be repaired or replicated. As we shall see, it may be that the higher value of a historic building justifies the higher costs of refurbishment. But where a mix of old buildings within an existing street pattern is concerned, the balance of costs and development value often work against such large-scale refurbishment. A particularly challenging planning task is to facilitate development to promote the prosperity of an area while maintaining valued historic features.

One key resource that planning systems have in seeking to secure the conservation of urban heritage is not information about the value of older buildings and areas nor a vision for how they could enhance

—

the visual appeal and economic prosperity of an area – important as those are. Rather, it is the enhanced regulatory control that comes with identifying buildings and areas as historic. Planning regulation here is about more than just saying 'yes' or 'no' to development proposals. It is also about regulating the detailed form of that development on both an individual and area basis.

Such regulation can operate on a building-by-building basis. In the UK, historic buildings are 'listed', that is, put on a list with a rating to identify just how historically important they are. They then become subject to much more detailed and intensive control over any proposed changes, as well as requiring specific permission for demolition. Alternatively, regulation can operate on an area basis. Again in the UK, 'conservation areas' can be designated on the basis of their particular contribution to urban heritage. This results in much greater information about the area and its characteristics being collected to inform planning and development decisions there. It supports an area-management approach in which policies are set out for managing the area as a whole, including the impact of new development proposals.

This approach of trying to meld the best of the existing built environment with an improved form of new development can be applied outside of such designated areas. Planning can seek to use existing built heritage and incorporate it within plans for change wherever valued buildings are found. The rationale is not just about aesthetic sensitivities to existing built form, it is also about capitalising on the social connections that the existing built environment allows or even fosters. And it is about using those existing assets to support a form of place-making that will create a better local environment and potentially attract more people and businesses to the area.[13]

This framework offers planners scope for preventing inappropriate development and using regulation to influence the quality and nature of any development that is permitted. However, such a framework does nothing to ensure that the existing built fabric is maintained; without this, older buildings and even whole areas can fall into disrepair and decay. Indeed, wary of the costs of maintaining older buildings and of the limitations on development, potential, unscrupulous owners of listed buildings have been known to let them fall into such disrepair that they are considered no longer worthy of listing and then ripe for demolition.

While some conservation frameworks require the owner of a historic building to keep it in good repair, this can be a difficult law to enforce. The economic truth is that resources are needed to ensure the historic urban fabric is properly cared for. This means public subsidies, either through the state or an organisation such as the National Trust, or a reliance on wealthy private organisations and individuals who have an interest in maintaining their properties for reasons of prestige or self-satisfaction. As we shall see, the latter route has some distinct drawbacks in terms of meeting broader planning goals for an area.

Another concern about the regulatory framework for historic buildings is that it may be inhibiting measures to improve the energy efficiency of the historic stock. This arises from the detail with which the regulation of older valued buildings is exercised and the tendency to favour replication of existing historic features. This approach can severely inhibit the ability to improve the energy efficiency of the existing historic stock. Where efficiency improvements are achieved, the costs of undertaking such retrofitting while ensuring that the building still looks the same down to small details of fixtures and fittings can be high. UCL and the London Borough of Camden cooperated on the refurbishment of a Victorian house to explore the technological and economic possibilities within the limits of conservation policies.[14] Double-glazing, insulation to the roof, walls and floors, solar thermal panels, solar photovoltaic (PV) panels and heat exchangers were installed. The cost (including consultancy fees but excluding the wall insulation, which was donated) came to about £52,500. External cladding was prohibited by planning regulation. The issue here is the extent to which planning regulation is inhibiting moves towards retrofitting historic buildings for sustainability by restricting the options for refurbishment.

Conserving landscapes and habitats

Heritage is not just found in built settlements, however. Landscapes are also valued features of our environment. They often have historic importance, as with battlefield sites, but they are also highly significant in cultural terms. As discussed previously, national and regional identity can be closely tied up with the appreciation of a landscape. Even in highly urbanised countries, most of the land still counts as rural. In the UK in 2001, nearly 80% of the population lived in urban areas, but less than 9% of the area was under urban development.[15] So rural land is a considerable feature in all countries other than highly urbanised island states.

The role that planning can play in protecting such areas is rather different from that in the case of urban conservation. There is an amenity dimension; the countryside is valued for its beauty and for views, both routine and spectacular. This has led to planning approaches that seek to protect such views by constraining development in rural locations generally and exercising heavy controls in places of particular beauty. Designations of all sorts are used to guide decisions on where development should or should not go, such as Areas of Outstanding Natural Beauty or Areas of Special Landscape Value.

But rural conservation is not just about protecting views. Access to the countryside is also important so that people can enjoy those views and, furthermore, the pleasure of being physically within the rural environment. For many cultures, engagement with rurality has a deep, even spiritual meaning. In the West, the cultural movements of transcendentalism and romanticism capture this, with their idea of a person being transformed by direct involvement with nature.[16]

Yet access is a more contested issue than visual amenity, because access requires crossing land that might belong to others and be in productive use. In England, a key point in the campaign for access to the countryside was a mass trespass, largely by urban working-class ramblers, on land at Kinderscout in the Peak District in 1932. Some countries have enshrined a general right of access into legislation. Sweden has a concept called *Allemansratt*, which means that anyone can cross any land provided that no harm is done. In the US, the designation of National Parks confirms these areas as public land to which everyone has a right of access; this contrasts with National Parks in the UK, where private property ownership remains unchanged by designation and access is therefore dependent

—

on public rights of way for specific paths or designated areas. In the UK, there has traditionally been a heavy dependence for public access on landowning bodies such as the National Trust and the Woodland Trust. This changed in 2000 with the Countryside and Rights of Way Act, which provides a new right of pedestrian public access to areas of open land comprising mountain, moor, heath, down, and registered common land subject to certain safeguards for farming and nature conservation interests.

Access is not just a matter of right, though. There can also be subtle cultural signals constraining the use that people make of such rights. In the UK, access to the countryside has historically been part of a struggle between wealthy landowners and the urban classes, particularly the working class living in dire urban circumstances. More recently it has been a conflict between farmers and urban dwellers of all kinds over traverse across cultivated land. The conflict centres on claims about who owns the land, and who has the right to use and enjoy it. Disputes of this kind extend to the issue of who feels comfortable using and enjoying the countryside. In particular, if the countryside is such a potent symbol of national identity, are there cultural barriers to certain ethnic groups accessing rural areas? Or, to put it more simply, how can access to the countryside be encouraged in a multicultural society? Mosaic is a project seeking to increase the number of ethnic minority visitors to the National Parks by recruiting Community Champions and developing local groups of such champions.[17]

Planning, therefore, has a role in maintaining the visual beauty of landscapes and at the same time encouraging access to and enjoyment of those landscapes. This may involve making difficult decisions where access and landscape protection conflict. Such decisions can become more difficult when a third role is added, that of protecting and enhancing biodiversity. Biodiversity is not confined to rural areas; there is a significant task of nature conservation within towns and cities.[18] But ensuring that the broad tracts of rural land are rich in biodiversity is essential for achieving overall nature conservation goals. Designation of both habitats and species are key planning tools to ensure that development and land use does not threaten rare flora and fauna. Nature reserves are a key area-based designation and they

—

come in all scales, from local pocket reserves to major areas of land and can be significant to biodiversity on a local, regional, national or even international scale.

Achieving the multiple goals of amenity, access and biodiversity involves more than just protecting land from development. It also involves decisions about how the countryside is managed. Management of land is a detailed and ongoing process in which the uses of land in different ways and by different groups – farmers, tourists and native species – have to be balanced against each other and sympathetic ways of maximising the benefits to all sought. This tends to go beyond the remit of a planning system. For example, European Union agricultural policy has shifted away from simply rewarding production to providing financial payments for land management practices that enhance nature conservation, and this is probably the major influence on how rural land is used and managed across Europe today.[19]

Deciding on management options is not just a technical issue, whether to reward this crop or that and how to frame the incentive. It is also a political issue, involving who should have a say about such management decisions. One of the difficulties here is the sheer number of interests involved in such decisions. There are productive interests in farming, forestry, fishing, water capture or mining, which may be organised on very different scales, from large-scale commercial agro-industry or international mining conglomerates to smaller farmers and, in some cases, self-sufficient agrarian communities. There are communities that live in these areas, who may or may not be involved in these productive industries, and there are the urban visitors to the area, coming for a mix of reasons. And then there are the expert organisations in the public and non-governmental sectors associated with biodiversity, resource management, amenity and heritage. Managing these different voices and their interaction is a complex task for planning.[20]

Conservation and the market

Conservation happens because people value certain townscapes and landscapes. But as the previous discussion has highlighted, these can be valued for many different reasons by many different people and organisations: for their visual amenity, access for leisure, place-making qualities, contribution to local economic development, historic heritage, meaningfulness to a local community or as habitats for flora and fauna. As has been stressed, whose valuations count affects which of these aspects will be taken into consideration.

One overriding difficulty with conservation is that is comes at a cost. Profitable activities may be prevented. Development that is permitted is more costly than would otherwise be the case. And ongoing maintenance and management consumes resources, although in some cases these may be provided on a voluntary basis by community groups. For this reason, conservation either has to rely on funding from the public sector or the resources (often contribution in kind) from a non-governmental organisation (NGO), or engage with the economics of the market-place. This means using the potential of the market to generate the profit for conservation activities. The potential of the market is uplifted in the case of conservation activities because the market sometimes places a positive economic value on heritage features.

Often development within a conservation area will carry a premium over and above the value of that development elsewhere and this premium may then pay for the extra development measures required to maintain the special qualities of that area. This process has been apparent in the King's Cross/St Pancras regeneration in London.[21] Another example is an initiative for bringing tourists to a rural estate to finance the upkeep of an historic building and rural landscape. The quantity of funds produced will depend on the market demand for and consumer valuation of the features of the estate.

The danger with this approach is that the promotion of economic activity, which is financially underpinning the conservation activities, may itself threaten the very features that led people to value the area and buildings. So too much new development in an urban historic area, even if of the highest standard, may undermine the qualities that made that area attractive. Too many people visiting a rural estate will create erosion to the landscape, outstripping the ability of management practices to keep it in check. And encouraging

—

large numbers of people to the area may mean that the tranquillity associated with such rural estates is also eroded.

Another outcome of this kind of market-led conservation operating within a tight regulatory framework, particularly where built heritage is concerned, is that it conserves the built fabric but at the cost of any authentic feel of the history of the urban area and buildings. Conservation by means of development can result in a form of mock-historic urbanism that negates the purpose of conservation. A historic area needs to be functional in modern-day terms to avoid being a museum but it also needs to avoid being sanitised by conservation-controlled new development. This is a fine line that conservation planning needs to negotiate.

However, the gravest concern with this approach is the disregard of social inequalities that can result from the interaction of conservation policies with property prices. This goes back to the point made earlier that some of the features that are valued in heritage areas and landscapes are captured through market processes and capitalised into the price of property. So houses in national parks and similar countryside designations are considerably more expensive than a similar property outside the designated area.[22] Thus all the effort that goes into countryside protection and enhancement may create an inflated local property market. This can cause considerable problems for local residents and especially for younger people within the area when they need to find a home of their own for the first time.

A similar effect can be seen in urban areas, where an older area is refurbished in a way that brings out the historic features. The resulting housing, located now within an area with such desirable features, will command higher prices and attract a different socioeconomic group. It may well be that property is now offered for sale when it was rented out previously. The social composition of the area changes. With the higher local incomes, a range of local facilities become viable, so that the local economy becomes more buoyant and prosperous. This process should count as a success story except that it ignores the people who were living in this run-down area before. They are effectively priced out of the local housing market and therefore unable to live locally or enjoy the fruit of the conservation efforts. In this way conservation drives the dark side of gentrification.[23]

—

A final concern about conservation policies in rural and urban areas is that they also tend to be inherently conservative. They look backwards to past times rather than forwards to the needs of future generations and this may impinge on how efforts towards sustainability proceed. The danger is that conservation may become a banner for inhibiting change and resisting innovation. For example, renewable energy schemes such as wind farms are resisted on the basis of the impact on landscape and micro-generation installations such as solar panels or photovoltaics are resisted on the basis of the impact on historic roof-lines. (The similar problems with retrofitting historic buildings to enhance energy efficiency have already been mentioned.)

But the choice need not be between maintaining heritage values and promoting sustainable ideas. The idea of what constitutes heritage value is not fixed. It depends on whose values are being discussed. Ideas of visual beauty also change over time; many of the rural areas that we now revere were seen as dirty and dangerous a few centuries ago. Even the category of the historically important is not immutable; new ideas about what should be conserved from a historic point of view also emerge over time. This means that innovations from a sustainability perspective can be considered compatible with the concepts informing conservation. It depends on the prevailing values: societal, community and professional values. The bigger danger is to see conservation as preservation, in other words, not allowing change; whereas conservation is about meeting certain values regarding urban and rural areas, values which are themselves always changing. Planning needs to be alert to these changing social values as it seeks to preserve the best of today's environment for the future.

SIX

Not in my back yard

The previous chapter discussed resistance to change in the name of conservation. NIMBYism (or 'not in my back yard'-ism) is the term coined for the negative side to such resistance. NIMBYism has a bad name. It stands for a selfish attitude, protesting against development in the vicinity of one's own home without caring where the development would otherwise go. Numerous public protests against all sorts of development – housebuilding, waste facilities, airports – have been labelled NIMBY and thus cast in a negative light. Is this such an unreasonable approach? What causes NIMBYism and why is it a bad idea? How does it relate to the idea of the public interest? And where does it leave ideas for encouraging public participation in planning?

The causes of NIMBYism

It would be simple to answer the question of the causes of NIMBYism with the statement that people are defending their own economic interests by engaging in NIMBYism and opposing developments in their locality. And this is part of the answer. As the discussion in previous chapters has emphasised, planning is centrally concerned with the impact of development on people's interests, but not just economic interests, important as they are. The earlier discussion also highlighted how people's values and lifestyles are tied up in their attitude to new development. The simpler debates about NIMBYism run the risk of only using this label when the interests, values and lifestyles of those people involved do not seem worthy of support.

But NIMBYism is just a form – quite a common form – that public engagement with the planning system takes. Where people protest against development proposals they are exercising their right to participate in the planning process and express their point of view.

—

Since the 1960s it has been considered important that people should have a say in decisions that affect them. Therefore the planning system offers a range of opportunities for such participation: responses to consultation exercises, attendance at public meetings, letter and local media campaigns, lobbying of local politicians, attendance at local public inquiries into development proposals, and so on.

Sometimes these protests go beyond the usual procedural avenues and become forms of direct action, such as marches or even illegal occupation of sites.[1] The scale of such activism on the part of local communities is testimony to the ability of a NIMBY perspective to generate strong feelings. Perhaps it is not surprising that people take this kind of action when they feel that a new development would impact negatively on them. But there is also something in the dynamics of NIMBY politics that generates such consolidated action.

Anti-development protests are one of the few forms of collective action most likely to achieve significant levels of involvement from local communities on a sustained basis.[2] This is because people can see a threat to their quality of life and the economic value of their property that is both immediate and certain. All the factors that usually inhibit public engagement in policy issues – the costs of the time and effort involved and the small likelihood of having an impact on the development decision – pale into insignificance in the face of these threats.

Added to this, such protests are often spurred on by the close social ties that exist within a community, ties which themselves can become closer in a community that sees itself as under threat. Neighbour encourages neighbour to join in the protest in these circumstances, and neighbours see themselves as having something in common because of the development threat. The conflict with the development proponents further fosters the sense of a common identity among local residents. Given the area-based nature of the development impacts, it is likely that the people affected will already have much in common and may even form a coherent group. Local housing markets tend to sort people into such groups. But the dynamics of a local anti-development protest group are likely to enhance this and reinforce the pressures for NIMBYism.

—

This kind of political action, even when invited by the participatory processes of the planning system, is often viewed unsympathetically. Such protest is labelled selfish, but protest on behalf of the local community can only be seen as selfish when weighed against some broader sense of collective benefit. A number of arguments have been made for overcoming local opposition to development in the name of this broader collective benefit or public interest.

The idea of the public interest lies at the root of the justification for most public policy and certainly has a key role in the historic rationale for planning. Planning is supposed to be, above all, about promoting the public interest. However, this can be very difficult to define and much depends on how the problems and issues of the time are framed. There are a number of different forms in which the public interest can be invoked: national interest, regional interest, social cohesion and sustainable development.

NIMBYism and the public interest

The national interest

There tend to be two framings used to define the public interest as the national interest. The first of these is economic. Behind this framing is the idea that promoting economic activity is of primary importance to ensuring the wealth, health and happiness of society. Such economic activity, it is argued, is essential for the maintenance and improvement of standards of living, for the creation of wealth out of which public services can be funded and for the possibility of redressing inequalities within society.

Economic activity usually generates some benefits at the level of the region or locality where the development will occur – employment, increased spending power, orders for local firms – and this might be assumed to create some level of support within local communities. But, so this argument runs, local economic activity has to be seen in the context of the national economy. Regional or local economies are not divorced from each other or, more importantly, the national economic context. And the concept of the national interest tends to have the national economy at its heart. On this basis, it can be argued

—

that it is in the national interest to allow development in a locality even against the wishes of local residents.

In England during the 1990s and 2000s, the explicit view of the New Labour government was that the South East of the country was the economic powerhouse of the national economy. Therefore, it was argued, there was a need to allow development in that region even when many felt that the region was already overdeveloped in relation to the local infrastructure and in comparison with other regions. The government's Sustainable Communities Plan put the main growth into four areas within a 100-mile radius around London: the massive Thames Gateway development along the river; Ashford in Kent, on the route of the Channel Tunnel rail-link; the former new town of Milton Keynes, which had never been fully built out; and the M11 corridor leading up to Cambridge.[3] Similar arguments are used to support development of infrastructure (such as roads, airports and power stations) deemed essential for economic activity. The third runway at Heathrow Airport was supported by the New Labour government over local opposition on this basis, but it was subsequently cancelled by the incoming coalition government in 2010.[4]

The second framing of the national interest, which has always been significant but has achieved greater importance since the events of 11 September 2001, concerns national security. Where a development is considered essential for reasons of national security, then this need is seen as outweighing local considerations. Military installations are clearly one example of such security requirements. But the argument has also been extended to a broader understanding of national security as a result of geopolitical shifts threatening the supply of energy.[5] Here arguments about the national economic interest overlap and reinforce arguments about national security, supporting development in energy infrastructure.

As a result national governments promote power stations, oil and gas pipelines and energy networks regardless of local concerns. A new programme of nuclear power stations has been planned in the UK on this basis.[6] The need to get such nationally important infrastructure through the processes of the planning system has often curtailed the scope for giving voice to local opposition, that is, to NIMBYism.

—

In the past, public inquiries were held into such infrastructure proposals but the procedures curtailed the debate to issues of siting, landscaping, and so on rather than testing the arguments about the need for such installations.[7] Nevertheless such inquiries did offer opportunities for NIMBY protest. More recently, an Infrastructure Planning Commission has been set up to consider such proposals with a streamlined process that explicitly limits the opportunities for public expression of opposition.[8] (This Commission is likely to be absorbed into the Planning Inspectorate.) National Policy Statements will set out the general framework for such infrastructure including the arguments about need.

The regional interest

Local concerns about development are also overturned in the name of the collective interest at the regional level. Planning systems often take a view on the amount of desirable development not just in specific locations, but at successive scales. This has been discussed in Chapter Three in terms of the regional and local planning of quantities of housebuilding. But the concept applies to many types of development where there is a need to assess how much is appropriate for the regional or sub-regional scale, for example, transport or renewable energy. Once this has been decided, then decisions about development at more local levels have to be taken within this context. If all localities were to refuse to allow development to go ahead then clearly any regional and sub-regional totals would not be reached.

One example of this is the planning of waste treatment facilities.[9] In an attempt to manage waste more efficiently and sustainably, more societies are adopting policies of self-sufficiency in relation to waste treatment and disposal and, furthermore, adopting this at the regional scale. This means that a region has to deal with an increasing proportion of the waste that it generates within its own borders; it cannot solve its waste problem by exporting it to landfill sites or incinerators in other regions. This in turn puts a burden on the planning system within the region to find sufficient locations for waste treatment facilities, typically incinerators, but also for other treatments such as anaerobic digestion, pyrolysis and gasification.

—

These kinds of treatment facilities are typical LULUs (Locally Unwanted Land Uses) and unlikely to be desired by a local community. Fulfilling the self-sufficiency goal and meeting regional waste treatment targets may then require the location of treatment facilities being imposed on local communities. Without this kind of planning for waste treatment facilities across a region, waste may have to be transported considerable distances. Alternatively, it may be that only some communities are able to resist the pressure for such facilities, so that there are a few facilities across the region, often in areas where there is a precedent in favour of their location, creating waste treatment ghettos. This may create a suboptimal pattern of investment with waste being transported across the region. The scale of waste treatment plants will also be influenced by the limited number of places where permission can be obtained, so that there is a push to larger plants, when this may not be the optimal scale for facilities from an efficiency perspective, particularly the carbon efficiency of different waste treatment options.

Social cohesion

The third reason for overcoming local opposition to development is of rather a different kind. It relates less to the public interest being interpreted across different scales of planning (national, regional and local) and more about the norms that a society wishes to adopt in relation to social diversity. It is a shameful fact that, in any society, there are social groups that are subject to discrimination and seen as bad neighbours. Locating accommodation for such groups within an established community can lead to protest. It is sadly all too easy to find examples of such prejudice: the difficulty of finding sites for Romany or traveller families, resistance to hostels for asylum seekers, opposition to a mosque or synagogue, and so on. The underlying problem here is that protests against certain kinds of development are actually protests against the specific people involved. This can be an aspect of any anti-housebuilding protest where existing residents argue that the incomers would not understand the local way of life. Such protests can verge on, and indeed become, racist.

In these cases the role of planning is to represent publicly social norms regarding how such groups should be treated. Local opposition is ignored in order to establish clearly that such prejudice is unacceptable. Perhaps in this case it is reasonable to see NIMBYism as entirely a negative feature and something that should be wholeheartedly resisted. This links the arguments about local developments to debates about social coherence, multiculturalism and diversity. And any liberal framing of these debates would be seeking to change attitudes away from NIMBYism by raising the bigger issues that are involved.

By linking such local NIMBY protests to the wider issue of how society treats different groups and handles diversity, it may then be possible to alter the terms of the debate about a specific development and perhaps change local attitudes. An example of this occurred in 2007, when local residents in Ashtead, Surrey, a wealthy village in South East England, objected to the conversion of a building into a hostel for the families of wounded soldiers who were being treated in a nearby army hospital. Objections were on the basis of traffic and disruption of quiet village life but it was clear that there was also social discrimination at work here. The families of solders were of a different class to the village residents. When the media linked this protest into the broader debates about how veterans were being treated in British society during a period of active military service overseas, the debate altered; indeed, the development in this case was permitted. In this context, the current UK government's decision to remove the requirement on local authorities to find sites for traveller communities is disturbing.

Sustainable development

Sustainable development has been increasingly adopted as a dominant policy goal.[10] This also reframes the arguments about NIMBYism and the national economic interest. The argument that development proposals should be allowed in the interests of broader economic development depends on the assumption that market processes are the appropriate driver for economic development and on an acceptance of the consequences of relying on a version of market capitalism. It

—

also assumes that social goals can best be met from economic growth, which, in turn, is seen as driving up standards of living.

However, there is a critique of this argument that can be harnessed to anti-development protests to present a rather different view of social progress. In this critique the reliance on market capitalism itself is questioned. This need not be a wholesale call for an alternative social system, as in radical left-wing thought.[11] Rather, it is a sceptical attitude towards the presumed benefits of every market-driven development proposal. Associated with this is a redefinition of the goal of public policy away from economic growth towards a more broadly understood notion of economic development. In line with this, improved standards of living are not seen as the primary aim but rather enhanced quality of life. And this suggests that market-based monetary value is not always the best currency for judging whether people are living better lives.

The sustainability argument frames the opposition to development proposals within a broader case for the public good. Here the concept of the public good is seen in terms of the long-term sustainability of the planet, encompassing ideas of equity and the need for economic development but emphasising particularly the need to live within the limits of the earth's environmental resources and services. Thinking about sustainability takes a variety of forms, variously termed 'deep' or 'light' or 'strong' or 'weak'.[12] At the light and weak end, there is a greater tolerance of economic development as necessary for meeting societal needs and generating economic wealth for redistribution and investment. At the deep and strong end, there is an overriding concern that such development may breach the capacity of environmental systems and lead to irreversible and catastrophic environmental damage, drastically reducing humankind's life chances.

While the deep and strong perspective can turn NIMBYism into BANANA (Build Absolutely Nothing Anywhere Near Anyone), the weak and light end of the sustainability spectrum is clearly closer to prevailing political and social discourses, which argue that there is a need for further development. Framed within a sustainability discourse, however, the question is not "Where should this development go – your back yard or mine?". Rather, the sustainability focus raises different questions about whether the development

—

is necessary and whether other changes can be made that would render it less necessary or less unacceptable. These changes could be different ways of producing goods, with less toxic by-products or carbon emissions, or different ways of living that consume less resources and produce less waste.

Seen in this light NIMBYism becomes a spur to thinking hard about how society and the economy work and to finding different ways of living and producing that are less environmentally burdensome. To some extent this shift in thinking has occurred within the environmental justice movement in the US.[13] This social movement was built on the twin pillars of protest against locating toxic waste sites near residential development and the infrastructure of the civil rights movement, the two joined together by the finding that the majority of such housing was occupied by peoples of colour. What began as an anti-development protest moved into new arenas of debate as questions were raised as to why so much toxic waste was being produced and why industry was not trying to reduce these outputs at source, that is, within the factories. Explicit links to the sustainability agenda were drawn, connecting this specific environmental justice movement to a much broader range of campaigns against social and environmental injustice across the globe.[14]

Engaging communities

Linking NIMBY concerns to these broader social debates raises the question of how discussions about new development take place and the role of local communities in those discussions. The current dominant approach could be described as 'Decide and Defend' or DAD. Here the location of a particular development is announced and then the public discussions are structured around the defence of this.

DAD structures of debate and NIMBYism tend to go hand in hand. In the crudest forms of this approach there is little scope for public consultation to influence the development decision and as a result local politics has no real option but to become oppositional; there is little prospect of a more constructive approach reaping any rewards. The existence of formal avenues for community consultation within the planning system may provide the route for NIMBYism to be expressed. But the lack of response to community views expressed through these avenues may also move the opposition into the realm of direct action such as marches, sit-downs on the development site and other media events.

Sometimes proponents of a development and local communities may disagree as to whether the decision has been finally taken or not. The government may argue that a specific forum is a genuine opportunity to debate the development, while others suspect that the decision has already been taken. This difference of view is particularly fostered where there is an attempt to draw a line between those issues that can be debated at the forum and those that cannot. With developments where the national interest is being invoked, there is often an attempt to restrict debate on the principle of the development and only allow it on the details of whether this is the best site and how development impacts at this site could be mitigated. In such circumstances, NIMBYism is often fostered rather than assuaged.

Moving beyond DAD involves considering how the different groups and people with an interest in the development decision should engage with each other and contribute to the final decision. There are a number of different aspects to such opportunities for debating development decisions: the scope of those discussions (geographically, temporally and in terms of issues covered); the range of actors who will be involved and their role in the discussions; and the way in which interactions are managed. How these aspects are handled in any particular case determines the nature of the discussion and whether it remains narrowly NIMBYist in structure or opens out to something fuller and more productive.

Broadening out the scope of the discussion is central to the transformation of a narrow NIMBYist debate into one that addresses concerns about the public interest. Broadening the debate is not just about taking a different set of concerns into account; it can also involve considering a broader geographical scale and a long temporal horizon. This is essentially about moving from a development-specific debate to considering the strategic issues raised by such development – whether housebuilding, new retail facilities, waste treatment plants or power stations – and assessing these strategic issues from a variety

—

of perspectives, over different scales and for both present and future generations.

Such strategic thinking is the essence of spatial planning, recently established as the basis of UK planning, fitting in with trends found at the European level and in other locations (as discussed in Chapter Two). Such spatial planning distinguishes itself from town and country planning, development planning or land-use planning by focusing less on the particular patterns of land use or of development activity and instead looking at the desired patterns of economic and social activity across space. Chapter Two emphasised that spatial planning looks particularly at the role of infrastructure and public services in setting the framework for such activity and highlights the need to integrate infrastructure, public services and development as they change into the future.

Spatial planning is also about what these patterns of economic and social activity should look like in the future. It involves considering alternative future pathways rather than assuming that a continuation of present paths is inevitable. As such it offers the potential for raising challenging sets of questions that can reduce the influence of NIMBYist thinking within planning debates by questioning the needs for certain developments, the existing modes of production and retailing activity in an area and the way that diversity is viewed locally.

Such an approach is not without its difficulties, though (as has been mentioned in Chapter Two). First, integrating the plans of many different stakeholders within different sectors is essential for such a vision of spatial planning to be achieved. However, this takes time and the commitment of the different stakeholders in the different sectors, and may be constrained by conflicts of interest and limited resources. A focus on integration also throws the emphasis onto the involvement of those holding key resources for investment in infrastructure, public services and development. This may result in the exclusion of existing communities, who become framed as passive recipients of the new patterns of activity rather than key instigators.

Second, while the idea of a spatial local vision implies a creative process of considering a wide range of options for an area, in practice this tends to be constrained, not least by the visions of governmental authorities at higher tiers. If central government has a particular idea of change at the national level, then this will limit the options available for discussion at regional and local levels. And again if regional government – where is exists – has created a distinctive idea of regional change, this will constrain the local level. In the context of such constraints, it is all too easy for discussion to revert to a NIMBYist frame.

Third, even with a well-debated local spatial vision, this is unlikely to replace debate on specific development proposals. This is partly because strategic level discussion always needs to be specified in more detail for implementation and this raises the prospect of reopening issues that might appear to have been resolved at the more strategic level. Some planning systems lay themselves more open to this possibility than others. The UK system, with its division between spatial planning and development control or management, embeds these dual spaces of debate within its structure.

While spatial planning has the potential to move outward from a NIMBYist form of community engagement, it does also have limitations in this regard. This is because of the dynamics that cause different people and organisations to get involved in planning debates. As indicated previously, strategic-level planning discussions tend to concentrate on institutional stakeholders with resources and leverage in implementation. This is not just a preference on the part of the spatial planners; it also reflects the preferences of local communities, who often find the discussion at a strategic level too general and uncertain to engage them. It is at the stage when implementation throws up the prospect of specific local changes occurring that local communities tend to get involved.

This can be understood in terms of the collective action problem that underpins all such engagement.[15] Actors will participate when they see the benefits of doing so outweighing the costs. Given that the costs of participation are certain, fall on specified people and fall on them in the present, getting involved in general discussions of what may happen in the future and may or may not affect a particular person or group is not that attractive. This is often reinforced by a sense that their individual participation is unlikely to result in concrete changes and that someone else can be relied on to represent the broader group of people. Only strong social norms in favour of

—

participation tend to alter the perceived balance of costs and benefits in favour of getting involved in such strategic discussions.

The impact of these dynamics tends to push debates on future development in two directions: towards relatively closed stakeholder-based discussions on broader strategic issues; and a more open discussion involving local communities on specific development proposals. This reinforces NIMBYist tendencies rather than making the links to broader debates that could rob NIMBYism of its more negative aspects.

There have, however, been attempts to create new forums for planning debates that would overcome such problems.[16] These forums look for ways of engaging communities and community representatives in a more forward-looking and open discussion. They have variously taken the form of citizens' juries, deliberative forums, planning for real exercises, and so on. The first aim for these debates is that they should be informed by a wide set of knowledge and information about the area, development options and the socioeconomic context. The second aim is that they should provide space for in-depth consideration, delving into deeply held values among the communities and allowing for opinions to be changed. This is in contrast to a consultation exercise that is set up to tap into existing views and may lead to them becoming more fixed and entrenched because there is no opportunity for debate.

However, the limitations of such exercises are twofold. First, they tend to involve a relatively small subset of the local community. This need not matter if the emphasis is on feeding community views into the decision-making process (and the assumption is that the views of the selected few somehow represent the wider community). If the aim is to include as much of the community as possible within a debate, some of these deliberative forums may backfire by appearing rather exclusionary. Second, it is not always clear how deliberation at such forums feeds into decision making. If there is not a clear link, then the exercise may seem purely tokenistic and not contribute to diluting NIMBYist feelings; instead it may seem just to cloak DAD in a new guise.

The difficulty is that NIMBYism derives its strength from the way that it taps into and exposes the very real conflicts that lie at the heart

—

of planning decision making. What is needed is a form of debate that is able to deal with such conflicts and the oppositional views that they generate. Deliberative approaches often aim at delivering consensus or agreement so that this can support decision making in an unproblematic way. But the reality is that debates needs to be able handle dissent and disagreement if they are to be at all helpful in shaping planning debates. The search is on for a form of planning debate that can do this without becoming entrenched in the anti-/pro-development dichotomy.

The role of local elected politicians

This account of how communities and other stakeholders engage in debate over planning of development has largely ignored the role of local politicians. Instead it has focused on the relationships between planning officers, communities and others with a stake in the development proposal. Yet the arena of representative democracy has a legitimate role in debating issues of public interest and deciding about new development.

One of the key features of planning debates is that they range across tiers of government. The tension between definitions of the public interest at national, regional and local scales has already been pointed out. But this is not just a conceptual issue of scale. Most countries operate with formal governmental authorities at some if not all of these scales. Governmental structures vary from country to country. In the UK, national government is supplemented by devolved administrations in Wales, Scotland and Northern Ireland and by local government, which (depending on location) can take the form of county and district councils or unitary councils. In London, the Greater London Authority is the upper-tier level of local government. All these bodies are elected but there is no elected tier of regional government: there are a range of regional bodies, some of which are currently being dismantled.

In London and 12 other local authorities, the local electorate also vote for a mayor; elsewhere the mayor is a purely ceremonial function. Mayoral systems are often claimed to have more legitimacy because they raise the level of involvement in local politics and put an individual in a position of personal accountability for local decision making. As such they are commonly found in the US and European systems such as France, and there are proposals for extending their application in the UK.[17]

Each of these elected local governments will have some vision of the collective interest and how it would be served or undermined by particular development patterns. Each of these visions will have a claim to legitimacy based on the fact that the representatives in each authority have been elected. The tensions between different visions of the collective interest among these different authorities can only be resolved by judging these claims to legitimacy.

In some governmental structures – and Sweden is a case in point here – the local level or *kommune* has significant legitimacy. There is a high turnout in local government elections and the *kommunes* have considerable power, including resources arising from a substantial share of the income tax raised in the locality. In other governmental structures legitimacy is harnessed more closely and restrictively to the central level. In the UK, for example, the ability of local government to raise funds is curtailed by national government, with its reserve powers of 'capping' the council tax or the local domestic property tax. Most of local government funding comes from national government grants and from the distribution of the non-domestic property tax, which is set by national government. At the same time, turnouts at local elections are low, reinforcing the relatively low status of local government within claims to legitimacy.

So the judgement as to whether a local position on development is NIMBYist because it ignores other legitimate arguments for the development in the broader public interest also depends on where within governmental structures the balance of legitimacy lies. This is very much a societal judgement in specific contexts.

One feature that has undermined the ability of local government to argue that it should be the legitimate focus of decision-making power is the accusation that it is more open to undue influence, particularly where local politicians have some degree of control over planning decisions and use it on behalf of specific interests. The influence of local councillors on planning occurs through local authority planning committees, which mainly deal with larger developments, although

Local Review Boards have been established in Scotland to deal with appeals against decisions on minor developments. This influence can be both pro- and anti-development in nature.[18]

As discussed in Chapter Four, the planning system allocates development value to sites through its regulation of development permission. This can be worth a considerable amount of money and there is therefore a temptation for local landowners to try and influence local politicians so as to manipulate where this development permission will be given. Such links between local politicians and developers are not unknown, with development being promoted because it benefits the local politician as well as the developer. Clearly such influence is undesirable, bordering on corruption. Ensuring transparency and accountability in planning processes, particularly decision making that permits profitable development, is a vital check against such undue influence.[19]

On the other hand, the nature of local politics means that local politicians need to take account of the concerns of their local constituents, and particularly the most vocal of local constituents. They will see it as their role to represent these very localised concerns when exercising their influence over local planning. After all, the chance of a local politician being re-elected depends on these constituents. This can become another route for NIMBYist attitudes to enter planning debates. Most local planners will have stories to tell of where the balance of all the factors was clearly in favour of a particular development but a key local politician on a planning committee steadfastly opposed the development because of representations by his or her local constituents.

This might suggest that awarding considerable legitimacy to the most local level of government is a mistake if it is so prone to influence from developers, landowners and residents. While these influences may pull in different directions in terms of being pro- or anti-development, when put together they certainly contribute to embedding the NIMBYist frame of discussion about planning issues. But then there are arguments that similar pressures operate at non-local levels of representative democracy. Studies have often argued that major development interests have undue influence within national government circles, and indeed some developments may be being promoted directly by national government in the case, say, of infrastructure developments. On the other hand, national governments have also been known to pay particular regard to the anti-development views of certain communities, where the votes of those communities in marginal constituencies may be significant in electoral terms for keeping a government in power.

The main conclusion that can be drawn is that there is a range of reasons why NIMBYist arguments frame the discussion of many planning debates. This is not so easy to change. What is needed is a broader form of discussion about development and how it contributes to societal goals. Perhaps the biggest indictment of representative democracy is that it has not always contributed sufficiently to such broader discussion about planning issues.

SEVEN

My home is my castle

In the previous chapter the role of planning when faced with local communities objecting to development was explored. In this one, attention turns to how planning should handle cases where people want to undertake development regarding their own home and often resent interference from the state. How does planning relate to these domestic property rights? What is the relationship between private and collective interests when households are the ones seeking rather than resisting development? And how can planning assist in making households more sustainable?

The distinctiveness of home-based development

If local environments carry significance for local communities, homes carry even more for families and households.[1] They represent the meeting of one of our most basic needs – the need for shelter. But they are much more than that. They are the location for relationships within families – the most potent relationships there are – and they are central to friendship circles. They offer scope for self-expression and creating a space that represents oneself and one's lifestyle. At a social level, the idea of the home is a very powerful one, symbolising rootedness, safety and autonomy. Such societal myths have an impact, regardless of what life is actually like within the millions of homes in a country. They suggest what life should be like and as such drive our attempts to shape our own lives and the immediate environment we live within.

A home will carry a household through part of its life-cycle, adapting as time passes and new requirements are made of its physical fabric. If lived in for any time, a home is a storage vessel for millions of memories. It has meaning for the people who live and have lived there. Such attachment to a home is more likely to increase with the time that has been spent there and the degree of choice that was involved in moving into or staying in the home. Those who move frequently and whose housing choices are imposed may well have less invested emotionally in their physical home. Those who have just moved into the house of their dreams will view it quite differently.

This is only partly a matter of the economic investment in the home. In some countries (as mentioned in Chapter Two) owner-occupation is the norm and attitudes to the home will be affected by the investment potential that owner-occupation carries.[2] But in other countries, long-term renting is common. Here there is no reason to assume that the emotional attachment to the home is any less. But the economic interest will be different and there will be the relationship with the landlord (private individual, company, housing association or local authority) to consider. In the case of owner-occupation, the household may wish to develop their property in some way to meet their family needs but also enhance its value. In the case of rented housing, landlords and tenants will have to negotiate over any changes to the property, with who has the dominant say depending on the legal contract between the two parties.

For all these reasons, any controls on what a household or homeowner may do with their home are contentious. We like to use our homes as an expression of who we are and interference with this is keenly felt. We do not expect the state to tell us how to decorate the interior of our homes and where to put our books and pictures. So why do we accept some control of how we handle the exterior of our homes and whether we can physically change them? What is involved here is a different form of the relationship between private and collective interest, between the desires and needs of the household and the public interest as variously understood. To explore this, it is necessary to consider how the household, based in its home, relates to immediate neighbours and to the broader neighbourhood.

Home and the neighbours

Homes do not exist in isolation. Outside of rural areas, most homes are found in close proximity to each other. Thus debates about what to do with one's home need to be seen in the context of what that means for neighbours and for relationships between neighbours.

Individual small changes to a dwelling can accumulate to change a local area significantly. If every house in a street goes in for stone-cladding, then the street looks different. Conversely, if one house makes a radical change, then that affects everyone who lives in the street and passes it. An unusual example of this is the glass-fibre, more-than-life-sized shark that the owner of a small terraced house in Oxford decided to put through the roof of his house and which has become a cause célèbre in English planning circles.[3] Neighbours may or may not like the changes that are being made in their neighbourhood. The questions are whether they should be controlled and who should control them.

The dominant approach within the planning system is to use regulatory powers as set down in development control policies or zoning ordinances to decide what kinds of development should or should not be allowed. To take an example, if a homeowner wants to erect an extension to his/her house that will impact on the view and light of the neighbours, then a planning system could potentially seek to control such development. In the UK, an extension above a certain size would need to go through a planning permission process to be assessed on all the impacts including those on the neighbours.[4] The neighbours would be consulted but would not have any special weight within the decision-making process, unless they put forward reasons that are recognised by the planning system. This situation often leaves people feeling powerless and frustrated. In other countries, detailed zoning ordinances would determine what was allowed and what was not in the case of such extensions.

Increasingly within England and Wales there has been a trend towards taking such small development proposals out of the planning system altogether. The main reason for this is that the very large numbers of applications for such development clog up the development control system. In 2008/09 householder applications accounted for 48% of all decisions.[5] This number increased considerably during the 1990s, an increase of about 125%.[6] About 90% of these applications are approved but not before considerable discussion, a site visit and officer deliberation. In response the Householder Development Consents

Review (HDCR) was set up in 2005. It reported in 2006, and this has led to a steady stream of amendments to the householder consent regime. In addition, as of April 2009, a streamlined Householder Appeals System was set up by the Planning Inspectorate to deal with disagreements between householders and local planning authorities over householder developments.[7]

These changes build on current provisions for reducing the number of applications that are considered by planners and planning committees in the UK. The General Development Order is a mechanism by which central government determines what householder developments can go ahead without specific planning permission. Under the Planning and Compulsory Purchase Act 2004, local councils in England and Wales can also develop their own variants by means of a Local Development Order.

Rather than tinker around with the regulatory aspects of planning, there is a school of thought that such decisions should be left to neighbours themselves to sort out.[8] This turns planning into the realm of property law. If a change to one home impacts on another then this should be decided through the two neighbours using their property rights to decide on the development. This is not just about each homeowner having an enhanced set of property rights so that she or he can do what they like with their home. Rather, it is about the property rights being defined so that if one neighbour undertakes a development that the other does not like, then the neighbours have to engage with each other over the issue and reach an agreement. This makes people think about the value to themselves and their neighbours of the change being proposed.

To return to the example of an extension to a residential property discussed earlier, if a property rights approach were adopted, then the rights held by each property owner would have to be redrawn to allow neighbours to have a legal say in what is permitted on adjoining land and what is not. It might be that certain development, say up to a certain size or for a certain function, would be allowed in all cases. Beyond that, the neighbour with development aspirations would need to get the permission of their neighbours before going ahead. The neighbour might simply exercise a veto, but there is also the possibility of compensation being paid for accepting that the development will go ahead. This puts a financial value on the benefits of the development and the nature of the impacts. It opens up the possibility of both parties leaving with something positive, the development on the one hand and a monetary sum on the other.

The limitation of a property rights approach is precisely that it only involves those with property rights and usually the more valuable property right trumps the lesser one. Thus if two owner-occupiers are engaging with each other over a development on one of their properties, a property-rights approach may work quite well. But if one of the properties is rented, then the owner-occupier of one dwelling will be negotiating with the landlord of the other. There may well be a difference of view about the development between the landlord and the tenant so that the final agreed solution may satisfy the landlord and the owner-occupier but not the residents of the tenanted property.

A third approach to dealing with such neighbourhood developments is to use the regulatory power of the planning system, but only to push the neighbours into mediation.[9] The essence of mediation is that a discussion between two parties can be framed so as to result in an outcome that, while a compromise, offers something to both sides. This involves recognition of the importance of letting both sides have their say, even if it is an angry and emotional say. The process of being allowed to say what one thinks in a safe environment is often very productive in itself; it can defuse the situation and allow the development issue to be seen in less emotionally charged terms.

Another element of mediation is the identification of the second-best outcome for each party and highlighting that it is often better to opt for such an outcome rather than risk all on pursuing the best outcome. Mediators manage the discussion between opposing parties to include a significant element of reality testing, identifying for each party the risks and consequences of not getting what one ideally wants as the outcome. In a planning case in the UK, this would involve emphasising to the potential developer the risks of not getting planning permission for the development, the costs of going to appeal (where the case would be heard and decided by a Planning Inspector) and the risks of losing that appeal. The householder would, in that circumstance, be out of pocket to a considerable degree and still not have the desired extension. For the neighbour the costs of participating in the appeal and the risks of the development going ahead with no potential for influencing it would also be emphasised. And for both there are the consequences of entrenching bad relations between neighbours, which could affect daily life. Mediation offers a way of avoiding all these costs and risks but it requires the regulatory force of the planning system to make it work.

Home and the neighbourhood

This discussion suggests that the planning system and associated property law can set the context for discussions between neighbours and thereby shape those relationships. But households do not just relate to their immediate neighbours; beyond this is the boundary of the neighbourhood. The idea of the neighbourhood involves a distinct spatial area of a certain number of homes together with some facilities such as a community centre, a few shops and/or a school. However, the neighbourhood also encompasses a sense of the environmental and visual character of an area, together with the networks of relationships between residents in the area. In thinking about planning and the home, there are the issues of how planning is involved in building these networks as well as protecting or enhancing local environmental quality.

When considering the networks of relationships between residents of an area, the term 'social capital' is often used (as has already been discussed in Chapter Three). This refers to the connections that exist within a community – with more frequent and dense connections building more social capital.[10] Some of these connections will be slight: knowing your neighbours' names and saying hallo in the street. But others will be more heavyweight, involving shared cups of coffee and turning acquaintances into friends. The significance of these types of connection is that they support certain norms of how to behave in the neighbourhood and in relation to neighbours.

The norms involved in social capital concern reciprocity, mutuality and trust. Reciprocity exists as a social mores when neighbourhoods offer to support each other in the knowledge that each favour will be repaid with another when needed. A classic neighbourhood context for reciprocity is at the school gates. Parents need each other to handle all the complexities of daily arrangement around family, school and work. If one parent will take another parent's child home after school, this can make all the difference. And the parent will do so knowing that the help will be returned if necessary, say when a morning school run is needed.

Such reciprocity is based on trust, particularly so where children are involved. But any informal system of favours and return of favours requires trust to work. Trust also makes a huge difference to a neighbourhood. Where neighbours trust each other then the sense of security in the local area is enhanced. People come to rely on each other for that security rather than investing in bars and gates and security devices. Neighbours can act as burglar alarms, noticing when something unusual is happening around a home. And this in turn generates a sense of well-being among the local community. Suspicion is wearing and not life-enhancing.

The third norm found in situations of considerable social capital is a sense of mutuality. This describes the sense that neighbours collectively feel that the neighbourhood is a common project. In this view, one's home is not just one's own personal castle to do with as one wants, perhaps limited by the opinions of immediate neighbours. Rather, one's home is part of the neighbourhood and cannot be seen as separate from that. What happens to the neighbourhood and how living in that neighbourhood feels day-by-day gives meaning to what happens in the home.

This turns the spotlight on the range of activities that seek to build social capital within a locality. In a large part this is about actively defining what it means to be part of a community. Community is a much-used word these days, trying to capture how people relate to their immediate social world. It tends to be linked to other markers of religion, class or ethnicity. And in highly divided societies, these markers may be so significant that community is defined by exclusion as much as inclusion. If you are a Muslim, you cannot be part of the Christian community; if you are working class, you cannot be part of the middle class; and so on.

However, in an increasingly globalised and mobile world this exclusionary view of community is be challenged by a more multicultural view of society in which people define their identity with reference to multiple communities. The white, middle-class and Christian communities do not exclusively map onto each other. Rather, people may be black, middle-class and Christian, or white, working-class and Muslim. This means that people have multiple identities and complex ways of relating across community boundaries. A local, neighbourhood community may be defined by a single set of markers, such as a Hispanic, Catholic, working-class area, but more typically the residents of an area will have a mix of identities particularly in relation to ethnicity, religion and class. This means that building a local community has to work with these multiple identities and the relationships between people with different self-identities.

Community building goes beyond the remit of most planning systems, but there is an important relationship in that neighbourhood-scale planning can contribute to a physical environment that fosters social capital. Local planning can ensure that space is found and development permitted for facilities which enable sub-communities to meet, both singly and with each other. Youth centres, community centres, places of worship and schools can all play this role. One use of planning gain (see Chapter Four) is to find the financial resources to provide capital funding for such facilities. Enabling and encouraging the use of these buildings around the clock, so that they meet the needs of different sectors of the community across the day and evening can then turn these physical buildings into social meeting spaces.

Planning also has a role to play in providing public spaces, designed to create other meeting points such as parks, allotments or city gardens. Increasingly it is recognised that the design of the public realm is a key factor in shaping the flow of people around a locality. And where people are walking and passing each other, there is scope for human contact, greeting and meeting. Urban design here involves creating high-quality spaces that people wish to visit and which evoke a sense of security so that people are not deterred from visiting.[11] It also involves privileging access and traverse by foot or other non-motorised means. Planning oriented around the pedestrian rather than the car is essential for fostering social capital within a neighbourhood.[12]

This means that traffic should be managed and streets planned to ensure that cars do not divide communities or take over the public space as throughways for those in vehicles. Research has repeatedly shown that contact between residents in a street is inversely related to the amount of traffic down that street.[13] The Dutch concept of the *woonerf* or play street is an example of how residential areas can be planned for local communities rather than cars, thereby fostering community relations.[14] In this concept, the car is either banned or given a subservient role. Speeds are dramatically reduced and physical barriers to driving through the street are built. Instead pavements are expanded and planting used to create pleasant environments, with seating and small play areas such as sandpits or slides.

A rather more mixed example of contemporary urban development, as far as community building is concerned, is the gated development. On the positive side, these have the potential to foster relationships between a close group of neighbours, by creating a common space for use as a garden or meeting point, a space which is secure and safe. This may take the form of a courtyard surrounded by walk-up flats or a garden surrounded by a mix of housing. Common management requirements may also act as a push factor towards building social capital within the development by requiring involvement in management committees and joint decision making on common spaces. This can supplement the pull factors created by the design of shared space.

Within such developments, communities may even be organised into a form of co-housing, sharing certain common facilities such as washing and drying areas.[15] In some cases, there may be joint eating facilities – a local canteen – as well as a nursery. These facilities will build closer bonds between residents and support them in their everyday lives. It has also been argued that such co-housing can enhance the sustainability of a residential development as well, reducing the energy and other resource consumption on a per capita basis.

However, the boundaries that create a sense of inclusion also create borders that exclude. A gated development separates housing from the surrounding area. Too many such developments may result in an imbalance between shared private space inside the gates and shared public space outside; social capital within the residential estate develops at the expense of social capital within the broader local community. Much depends, however, on how many gated developments there are, how the shared public space and streets are planned to encourage their common use and the culture of the local society. Many cultures have a tradition of shared courtyard developments that do not entirely separate residents from the local area, for example in mainland Europe and China. Therefore the issue is less about this particular building form than about the way that the entire local area is planned and used.

The importance of such neighbourhood planning is that by fostering social capital and building local communities, the relationships between neighbours will be changed. This will fundamentally alter attitudes to any individual project for changing a dwelling. It is not that all such changes will be automatically regarded as positive by neighbours; rather, that the processes of interaction between neighbours may prove more effective in reaching an acceptable compromise on such change. In effect, social capital internalises the mediation processes that otherwise a regulatory planning system may have to impose.

Home and sustainability

Sustainability and the home are closely interrelated. In the UK a quarter of all energy is used in the home.[16] In addition, homes are a primary site for water usage and their location determines many daily travel decisions, with consequent energy consumption. Gardens can be important sites of biodiversity within urban areas, and waste management at the level of the household influences recycling and composting rates.

For all these reasons, the sustainability agenda has become a key motivation for reconsidering planning and the home. The details of new housebuilding are increasingly being regulated with regard to sustainability concerns. The Code for Sustainable Homes provides a long list of features that should be provided in new homes to earn a higher sustainability rating, and increasingly these are being built into the regulations that control building standards.[17] The idea of mandatory building regulations has its origins in the desire to avoid unsafe building designs and poor construction work. This related not only to the physical robustness of the buildings but also to public health concerns. In particular, housing should be sanitary as well as physically sound. Now the sustainability agenda is expanding the scope of building regulation to reduce resource use in new build housing and promote more sustainable living through increased energy and water efficiency.

Regulation has also been used to promote renewable energy generation at the scale of the dwelling, either thermal energy through solar water panels, electricity through photovoltaic cells or a wind turbine, or methane through an anaerobic digestion unit. The Merton Rule was promoted within the UK in the early 21st century as a way of encouraging such micro-generation.[18] The Rule required a proportion (usually 10-20%) of residential development's energy needs or carbon emissions to be met by on-site renewable energy generation. (It also applied to non-residential development.) The aim was to stimulate the micro-generation industry through the widespread application of the Rule. More recently, the Merton Rule has been overtaken by the push towards demanding zero-carbon standards for all new housebuilding by 2016.[19] On-site micro-generation is one way of achieving such standards but there is also provision for 'allowable solutions' which incorporate additional off-site renewable energy generation into the calculation of whether a development counts as zero-carbon.

The difficulty with this approach to achieving a more sustainable housing sector is that new build makes only a marginal difference to the overall stock. The size of this difference obviously depends on the rate of new housebuilding compared with the stock, and this can be relatively low. In the UK, there is only a 1-2% addition to the housing stock resulting from new housebuilding each year. This means that tackling issues around sustainable housing also requires attention to the existing stock, that is, to existing homes.

Tackling the existing stock is not technically difficult.[20] The energy efficiency of a home can be readily improved by increased insulation in any loft space or added to the walls (internally in the case of cavity walls and through interior or exterior cladding in the case of solid walls). Double-glazing reduces heat loss through windows and even minor measures such a draught-proofing can make a substantial difference. Upgrading water-heating boilers to the latest technology and ensuring energy-using appliances are more efficient also contributes to reduced energy use. Similarly, water-saving measures can be readily retrofitted to taps, shower heads and toilets. Retrofitting equipment to generate energy is also feasible, although existing building layout and orientation may inhibit some options such as thermal solar panels.

The problem is how to incentivise such retrofitting. With new development, planning regulations can encourage or require amendments to design and construction plans. With existing stock this power is not usually available. There have been attempts to change English planning law so as to require such retrofitting when any amendment to an existing home is proposed but this was not enacted.[21] Such an approach has been adopted elsewhere, though. In 2008, Marburg became the first municipality in Germany to require solar thermal panels to be fitted when a building owner builds or renovates a building, fixes its roof or replaces its heating system. A similar ordinance is in place in Barcelona, Spain.[22] These measures suggest that more stringent and extensive regulation could be one way to improve the sustainability standards of current homes in the UK.

But a regulation-based approach to existing housing can be problematic. Regulation is only ever as good as its implementation, and this requires both monitoring and enforcement. These are aspects of a regulatory system that are typically under-resourced. Furthermore, regulation can lead to both perverse and undesired effects. A badly worded regulation may require certain measures, such as wind turbines, to be installed when they generate little electricity and their embodied carbon outstrips any carbon savings during the lifetime of the turbine.

Such regulation may also ignore the other considerations that planning seeks to take account of, such as the character of an area. Multiple wind turbines may destroy the appearance of a valued heritage area. Moreover, regulation may actually inhibit innovation if it takes a very rigid approach to what should be done and how. In Chapter Four, the way that strict conservation regulations may inhibit the ability to retrofit energy-efficiency measures was mentioned. Hence, outcomes-oriented regulations are more effective since they only stipulate the end result rather than the means by which that result should be achieved.

Of course, a heavy reliance on regulation also comes into direct conflict with the autonomy that many people particularly value with regard to their home. For this reason, there tends to be more of an emphasis on enabling and permitting retrofitting of existing homes rather than regulating for it. Sustainability can be promoted by allowing exemptions from regulation as well as imposing more stringent regulation. For example, the General Development Order (mentioned earlier) has been amended in order to allow micro-generation equipment to be fitted onto existing housing without the need for specific planning permission.

But such permissive moves are usually insufficient on their own to encourage retrofitting. Subsidies or financial incentives may be needed as well. For example, in England and Wales (as in many other European countries) households are now offered a 'feed-in tariff', whereby they are guaranteed a rate above the market price for any electricity that they generate through on-site renewable infrastructure.[23] The problem of relying on these measures is that take-up of resource efficiency measures by individual households has tended to be low, even when the payback period of the measure is relatively small and it would appear to make economic sense for a household to invest in them.

Quite why take-up should be low is not fully understood but it seems to be that people are inhibited by a mix of concerns over disturbance, poor workmanship and uncertain benefits.[24] There also seems to be a preference for the visible measures (such as micro wind turbines and solar panels) over the invisible (loft and cavity wall insulation) even though the latter may be much more effective. This does mean that relying on very large numbers of individual households to undertake such investments may not be a very effective way to achieve retrofitting. And tenanted properties create particular problems because the costs of installing such efficiency measures usually falls on the landlord, while it is the tenant who will benefit from lower fuel and water bills.

Most of these financial measures lie outside the remit of the planning system. However, there is a role for planning in encouraging and facilitating such retrofitting through area-based policy. This builds on the experiences that many planning systems have had in promoting area-based regeneration as an alternative to extensive clearance and redevelopment policies in the past. The essence of an area-based approach to retrofitting existing stock for sustainability is that additional benefits accrue from working on a number of dwellings at the same time, compared with working on them one by one at different times, and local planning can proactively manage such an approach.

The benefits of an area-based approach include economies of scale from buying in equipment, materials and labour in larger numbers. This can also be a way of ensuring that the investments in individual dwellings feed back into property values. There was always the concern with urban regeneration that improving an individual dwelling would not increase the value of that property because all the surrounding dwellings would remain unimproved, affecting perceptions of the local area. By improving all the dwellings together at the same time, it was hoped that the value of the area within the housing market would improve. In this way, a variety of house-based measures, such as re-roofing, double-glazing, and damp-proofing, went alongside area-based measures, such as improving paving and street furniture, tree planting and traffic management. This increased the attraction to households of permitting this work on their homes.

With sustainability improvements, action is less focused on improving value within the local market-place than on reducing energy and water consumption and associated costs. But given the resistance to such efficiency improvements, combining them with area improvement could be a way of ensuring that householders see that the costs of investment will be recouped, that disturbance will be minimised and good workmanship assured. There is also the potential for peer pressure to operate. And in lower income areas, area improvement can go beyond organisation of the retrofitting to the provision of subsidies. A further benefit of an area-based approach to retrofitting for sustainability is that it allows for measures that require a group of buildings to be connected together by a more energy-efficient and low-carbon means of energy and heat generation such as combined heat and power (CHP) and district heating.[25]

However, there is a caveat with all these changes to the building fabric – both new and existing – that planning can help to promote. At the end of the day, energy and other resource consumption depends on the behaviour of the people in those buildings, not on the buildings themselves.[26] The hope is that changes to the building fabric will influence this behaviour but people are very adept in finding ways of fulfilling their desires and wants despite the apparent constraints that the physical environment places on them.

This means that sustainable living within homes also depends on households changing their behaviour. Such behaviour is influenced by a range of social and economic factors. Clearly the price of resources has an effect but so do people's values in relation to resources and sustainability, the norms operating in the households and local community, the legal constraints of relationships to mortgage lenders and landlords, and the information that is available to people, say through billing and metering. Planning can have only a marginal impact on these factors. How people live within their homes is ultimately down to them and is within the remit of the autonomy of the domestic sphere.

EIGHT

The good life

The previous chapters have explored different aspects of the planning system and how it works. They have looked at strategic planning, planning allocations of land for residential development, urban regeneration and conservation, alongside public engagement and the concerns of individual households. Three general themes have emerged: the influence of market processes; the difficulties of community and stakeholder engagement; and the potential conflicts between public and private interests. This chapter reviews these key themes before returning to the title of the book, and discussing how they impact on the purpose of planning.

Planning and market dynamics

Market forces clearly play a significant role in shaping the outcomes of planning activities and, indeed, in also shaping the processes of planning. If the planning system has to rely on the private sector to deliver housing, urban regeneration or conservation, then planners have to engage directly with key personnel within the private sector. However, the private sector is driven by fundamentally different (if overlapping) interests from those of the planning system. It cannot be assumed that the private sector will deliver on planning goals; it may fail to address certain goals completely and may fulfil others only partially

The discussion of housing land provision, urban regeneration and conservation all highlighted the way that market processes are driven by purchasing power, with the result that the desired change in the built environment – the development of new houses, the transformation of an urban area, the preservation of the historic character of a locality – can all only be achieved by meeting the desires of those with the requisite finance available. Meeting new housing targets for an area relies on such housebuilding being profitable, for example.

This leads to uplifts in local land and property values being associated with success for the planning system. A regenerated urban area is one with more demand for local properties, driving up rents and property prices. Effective conservation policies will make property there more desirable and of higher value; similarly with good urban design policies. In a market-based economy, the desirable features of the built environment will be reflected in higher market values.

In addition, the planning system seeks to provide co-benefits from economic activity to meet social and environment goals. As the previous chapters have explained, much planning practice is based on the idea of leverage planning, namely that planning activity will bring in private sector investment that can be used to pay for a variety of such benefits to the community or broader public, often termed planning gain. The extraction of such planning gain is justified because the planning system itself, by its actions, has contributed to the change in land and development values.

Planning creates a higher-value local property market through promoting higher-quality urban design, ensuring a better arrangement of land uses, providing for the clustering of similar commercial uses where this brings economic benefits, avoiding land uses that devalue adjacent sites and prompting investment in infrastructure. But the regulatory aspects of planning also play a key role in unlocking higher land and development values through the grant of development permission. For these reasons, it is considered legitimate for the planning system to demand that some of the uplift in property values be used for wider community and social benefits.

In this approach, the costs of delivering these benefits fall on the developer in the first instance. They will then be reflected in lower land prices in the medium to long term, so that landowners eventually bear some of the cost. There may also be increases in prices for urban development, so that buyers and occupiers share the cost burden. But the intention is that in the long term the benefits to the local economy of better planning will produce increases in corporate and household income to offset some of these costs.

These kinds of interrelationship between planning and market processes allow market dynamics to underpin the delivery of certain planning goals but they also constrain what planning is able to achieve. In particular they limit the ability of the planning system to deliver benefits for those with less market purchasing power. Planning gain may provide some benefits – as with policies that require private developers to provide a proportion of affordable housing within their developments – but only where this can be done within the profit margins of the development.

To achieve these goals in weaker market circumstances or to deliver goals that are less compatible with profitable urban development and higher-value property markets will require the public sector to use its own financial resources. Regulatory resources are unlikely to be sufficient on their own. This may involve the use of land owned by the public sector, the sale of land at prices below market value or the use of powers of compulsory purchase to acquire and assemble land for private sector development. It may involve the public sector directly investing in infrastructure to create the right context for private sector activity: new roads, public transport links, energy systems, and so on. Alternatively, the public sector may fund or subsidise certain development, using its financial muscle to influence that development.

The message is that some such financial involvement by the public sector is an essential element for ensuring that planning goals are not undermined by market processes. The greater the resources that can be used to offset the influence of the market, the greater the chances of the public sector leading urban change and determining its outcomes. However, there are two caveats.

First, the planning system has to know how to use its financial power in relation to the pressures from market-based stakeholders. Otherwise, the benefits of those financial resources may just find their way into private sector pockets. Investing in infrastructure or providing cheap public land to developers may result in inflated development profits. Planners need to use these financial resources to extract more benefits for the public as a whole, or lower income groups in particular, and this puts demands on planners' bargaining abilities.

Second, giving more power within planning processes to the public sector raises the question of what kind of outcomes will result. Past experience with planner-led outcomes has suggested that for many the outcomes of market-led urban development are actually preferable. If an argument is to be built for using the resources of the public sector to guide urban change, then there needs to be confidence in the ability of planners to produce desirable change. This requires a mix of expertise on the part of planners about the most sustainable ways to future-proof urban areas, together with community engagement to understand what local people want from their built environment.

Planning and engagement with communities and stakeholders

The second general insight concerns the difficulties that are encountered with some of the claims for the planning system to be comprehensive in terms of public participation, community and stakeholder engagement, and, thereby, integration of different perspectives.

Public participation is hindered by the structural imbalance between what people can hope to get out of it and the costs of getting involved. It tends to be the campaigns against development proposals that most readily attract community involvement, based as they are in clear threats to people's interests and consolidated by the sense of common purpose. This means that it can be difficult to get public or community engagement in the more general forms of strategy development that planning undertakes. From the planner's perspective, it is the less welcome sides of public participation that are the most frequently offered.

Furthermore, getting a coherent viewpoint out of participation is constrained by all the fractures and cleavages within the notion of community. The term suggests something coherent, and yet engaging with 'the community' frequently just throws up multiple and often conflicting viewpoints. This leaves the planning system faced with the task of synthesising a vision for the locality or for urban development from the fundamentally un-synthesisable. These same two points also apply to stakeholder engagement. The planning system is faced with a variety of different interests, conflicting interests. Some will see no benefit in getting engaged with planning issues; others will do so only on the basis of promoting their own interests. The result can be a frustrating task for the planner.

The response to these problems of public, community and stakeholder engagement is to create a culture whereby people and organisations see it as an integral part of their role and identity to be involved in participatory exercises. Some countries are better than others in achieving this; it is perhaps not part of the public culture in the UK as yet. But it has been suggested that some steps towards such a culture can be achieved by building up social capital within local communities and among the networks of stakeholders with which planning wishes to engage. Such social capital can help to build relationships of trust, a sense of a common enterprise and a culture in which non-participation is viewed unfavourably.

Creating institutional structures like Local Strategic Partnerships can help to foster this sense of a local culture of participation among key stakeholders. Similarly, community-based institutions can encourage more positive planning consultation. However, it is probably wise to accept that many participatory exercises will struggle with participation fatigue, skewed patterns of involvement and the unwillingness to leave personal interest behind in favour of working towards the collective interest.

Involvement of stakeholders is also meant to be a path towards achieving integration of approaches and policies across different policy domains and government tiers. This draws on the knowledge and information that different stakeholders can bring to the planning process to promote an integrated solution. However, such integration can stumble on the cognitive demands of this exercise, namely the sheer amount of information and knowledge required to achieve this goal of spatial planning. In practice, rules of thumb have to be developed for what is a sufficient evidence base for integration to occur.

At the same time, planners will need to contend with the insights of knowledge and information from a variety of sources and in the context of the political pressures arising from the interests of the different stakeholders. For example, knowledge about the optimal pattern of waste treatment facilities across a locality and the most efficient scale for all those facilities given the current patterns of waste generation is needed to support integrated waste planning. But such planning will also need to deal with the political pressures arising from commercial waste interests, and from local communities and environmental groups pushing for and resisting the development of waste facilities in particular locations. Hence the calls so frequently made for planning practice to be firmly based on community and stakeholder engagement may bring as many problems as they do benefits to the planning exercise; in practice they are often seen as a necessity rather than a panacea.

Planning and the clash of public and private interests

Finally, it has been clear that the planning system continuously has to juggle its avowed intention to promote the public interest with the legitimate concern of individuals, households and firms about their interests, particularly their property-based interests. The domain of planning practice is a domain of conflicts of interest between different individuals, households and firms, on the one hand, and between these actors and the claim to a public or collective interest, on the other.

One of the roles for the planning system is the expression of this collective interest. However, it is not enough to assert a particular policy or decision as being in the public interest. This will never stop a disaffected party from claiming that their interest should prevail. Much will depend on the legitimacy of the planning system's claim to be the expression of the public interest. This will partly be rooted in the transparency, accountability and fairness of the procedures by which the planning system develops its plans and makes its decisions. Stakeholder and community involvement are therefore important in establishing a claim to legitimate planning. These processes of involvement may not produce consensus or compromise but they will bolster the claim to represent the collective interest in the face of conflict and discontent.

But one difficulty is that there is no single uncontested account of what counts as the public interest at any point in time. There will be debates about whether a certain level of regional growth would benefit the collectivity. There will be debates about what defines the collectivity: the locality, the region, the nation? There will be multiple alternatives for what counts as the public interest: regional economic growth, protection of regional landscapes, promotion of social inclusion, and so on. This diversity of visions for the collective good can give additional support to the claims of individual people and organisations that their own interests have been unfairly overridden. If there is no unanimity as to what counts as the public interest, how can it be appropriate to use the power of the public sector to deny private interests?

To be robust in the face of these claims for the primacy of private interests, the planning system needs not only legitimate procedures but also a coherent vision of what kind of outcomes, what kind of good life it is striving for. The need for this mix of both procedures that deliver legitimacy and a vision of what the future should be like has sometimes not been recognised sufficiently within writing on planning. Much theorising about planning has focused mainly on thinking about what the processes of planning should be like.

There has been an influential conversation between theorists such as Patsy Healey, Jean Hillier, Judith Innes, and Leonie Sandercock reflecting on the need to open up the processes of planning to a wider range of voices.[1] They have raised questions about whether certain people and groups are systematically ignored or undervalued in debates about plans and planning decisions. Detailed discussions have considered the institutional arrangements within planning and examined them to detect elements of bias. Suggestions have been made for enabling communication, encouraging deliberation, building consensus and handling conflict.

All these discussions are centrally concerned with creating a 'good' planning system. However, they largely operate with the assumption that if the procedures are right, the right outcomes will also result in terms of good plans, good decisions and a good built environment. This is more than assuming that planning outcomes will carry some legitimacy if the procedures are appropriate designed; this is making a judgement about the outcomes themselves and not just about how they are perceived.

The question is whether an emphasis on improving the procedures of planning results in a better place to live in. This is not straightforward. The procedures of planning ultimately determine which voice or voices get the biggest say in planning outcomes: plans, decisions and eventually change in the built environment. These procedures can structure which voices get access to planning discussions and which get heard: local communities, local businesses, housebuilders, vulnerable groups, public agencies, and the planners themselves. These procedures can also influence the way that urban change occurs, through different ways of influencing market processes: land purchase and supply, regulation, subsidies, and so on.

Thus the decision about what counts as a good planning procedure will influence whose vision of a good place prevails. Some planning commentators argue for a form of planning that gives more voice and power to the most economically and socially vulnerable groups.[2] Others favour an approach that would results in market actors driving plans, decision and change.[3] Others look to planners retaking central place within procedures to ensure that expertise leads investment in infrastructure and urban development.[4] So these forms of planning would lead to better forms of urban environment, if one is in agreement with the wishes and visions of the group favoured by those processes.

Often though, the aim of planning is seen as something larger than the voice of one actor or group of actors. The aim of planning is about balancing different voices and actors, not choosing between them but finding the right combination of viewpoints and suggestions for how urban development should occur. This is much more difficult because procedures that aim for balance, agreement, compromise or consensus among all the different parties to a planning debate can never be certain as to what the outcome of that debate will be. There is a danger that relying on planning procedures to determine the way that different voices and views will be combined to produce a plan or a decision abrogates any responsibility for thinking about the substance of urban change and the nature of the environment that people will live within.

If the planning system is to strive to deliver the good life, it needs more than the sense of good procedures properly carried out. It needs a sense of what the content as well as the processes of planning should be. This is not to suggest that the proponents of particular planning processes don't have views as to what they think the planning system should be achieving. There is usually a sense of what would be improved by the proposed approach, such as more economic activity if market actors are given more voice, or a better place for local communities if they are given more say. But this suggests that the planning system can do little more than give voice to the most important actors and this undermines the broader ways in which planners' expertise can contribute to this good life.

To explore this, a particular current definition of the good life – sustainable development – will be discussed. There is plenty of reference to sustainability in policy documentation and the public discourse more generally. This includes references within planning policy, from national legislation and planning policy guidance, through to requirements for its inclusion in numerous documents at the regional and local level, all framed by national-level strategy on sustainable development and on climate change.[5] This policy package makes a case for action in order to drive down the carbon emissions that are causing climate change, to put in place measures to help us cope with that climate change, to provide a sound economic basis for meeting employment and consumption needs and to generate a society that is inclusive and cohesive.

Thus there is a degree of legitimacy in basing the vision of the collective interest that planning activity should strive to achieve firmly within the sustainability frame. It provides an ethical base in terms of reducing the risks that vulnerable groups face from climate change at the same time as ensuring that the current generation makes a contribution to reducing the risks future generations will face from further climate change. It identifies the good life as one where people benefit from economic activity and no significant group of people is marginalised within society. It offers the prospect of a society bound by social capital in a way that underpins security and a sense of well-being within local communities.

If one takes the purpose of planning as being to deliver sustainability, then what does this mean for planning in practice? What aspects of this agenda is the planning system actually able to deliver on? The final section of the book discusses these issues, again using the three key themes of the role of market forces, the engagement with communities and stakeholders and the conflict between private and collective interests.

Planning for sustainable towns and cities

Market processes are going to have to play a role in delivering sustainable towns and cities. The question is what kind of role should they play, and what are the limitations of relying on the market to deliver sustainability. Relying on the interactions between the planning system and land markets to deliver sustainable outcomes fits with the paradigm known as ecological modernisation or green growth.[6] This model sees the potential for identifying win-win outcomes that both generate economic activity and also ensure environmental protection. Economic activity could be where the consumers demand a high standard of corporate environmental performance if they are to purchase the goods and services on offer, or it could be production of goods and services that are directly involved in environmental protection, such as clean-up technology, renewable energy services or carbon reduction consultancy.

While highly attractive as a way of delivering sustainability at the same time as economic growth, it presents some difficulties, particularly currently. The model is firmly based on the generation of market profit and hence on the purchasing power of consumers. Therefore it is threatened by any downturn in profitable economic activity. A temporary recession may pose such a threat, but the assumption will be that it can be waited out, with the normal model resuming once the economy has become more buoyant again.

But what if the downturn is not temporary but reflects a shift in the global pattern of economic activity? If the growth powerhouses in the global economy are China, Brazil, India and possibly Russia, where does that leave the countries that have been the global economic leaders in the past? Combined with demographic trends that predict population contraction in Europe (and hence an ageing population), this suggests that European countries may have to accommodate themselves to lower growth rates and therefore need a different planning model to deliver social and environmental benefits.

And, within a country, what if high levels of economic activity can only be assured within certain regions while other regions languish in the economic doldrums? Nations have had persistent difficulty in producing patterns of economic growth that reach all parts of the country. There tends to be a lead economic region, with the hope that growth will ripple out to reach other regions. However, regional inequality persists and, even in times of high national economic growth there can be substantial pockets of unemployment and associated deprivation. How is sustainable development to be delivered in all regions if it depends on economic growth?

Another increasingly important argument for rethinking the planning–economy interrelationship lies in the requirements for carbon reductions. The evidence is that the reliance on a modest adjustment to business-as-usual has been insufficient to drive carbon emissions down in the UK (or elsewhere).[7] The Kyoto Protocol committed the more developed countries to cuts in greenhouse gas emissions of about 5% over 1990 levels by 2010. However, global emissions have risen by 40% since 1990. It is now widely accepted that the Kyoto limits are insufficient to prevent dangerous climate change. The Fourth Assessment Report of the Intergovernmental Panel on Climate Change (IPCC) calls for a 450ppm target for carbon levels in the atmosphere to limit the global temperature increase to 2°C. This would mean a reduction in global emissions of up to 85% over 1990 levels by 2050.

Another assessment argues that by 2008 we had already used up a third of the carbon dioxide emissions budget for 2000–2050 that would give us a 75% chance of keeping the global temperature increase below 2°C. Therefore there will need to be considerable change to deliver the scale of carbon reductions that are now essential for climate protection. The longer that the attempt is made to deliver environmental sustainability through the current economic model, the bigger the challenge of carbon reduction that is being stored up.

The acknowledged requirement to make much deeper cuts in carbon emissions has implications for the kind of economic activity that is needed in the future. Jackson, in his powerful study *Prosperity without Growth*, talks about 'changing the engine of growth'[8] and focusing on 'low-carbon economic activities that employ people in ways that contribute meaningfully to human flourishing'.[9] Amongst these he counts a variety of local or community-based social enterprise activities: community energy projects, local farmers' markets, slow food cooperatives, sports clubs, libraries, community health and fitness centres, local repair and maintenance services, craft workshops, writing centres, water sports, community music and drama, local training and skills, yoga, hairdressing and gardening. He sees these as offering continued employment opportunities even as growth as measured by GDP falls and, furthermore, employment opportunities that offer meaningful and intrinsically valuable work.

In such an economy, the balance between consumption and investment would change, with less reliance on growth in consumption levels (and hence retail activity) and more emphasis on investment in innovative sectors of the economy. In line with the arguments of ecological modernisation, three areas for investment are specifically identified: resource efficiency measures such as waste reduction, energy efficiency and recycling; clean or low-carbon technologies such as renewable energy; and ecosystem enhancement such as climate adaptation, afforestation, wetland renewal, and so on. This would underpin an economy based on low growth and stable economic activity with commercial activity but also considerably more community-based activity.

So it may be that planning in the future – if it is to aspire to sustainability criteria – will need to consider how to deliver desired social and environmental outcomes in the face of a lack of growth or even de-growth (a newly emerging term). What would planning for sustainable de-growth look like? This is still not clear; the debate on this has hardly started. But, building on Jackson's vision, it would seem that using additional retail development as the basis of local economic development would be inappropriate. This would be a challenge to existing models of urban regeneration, particularly in city centres. Instead, the planning system would need to encourage development in green industries based on resource efficiency, waste reduction and low-carbon technologies. This pushes the planning system back to a task that it has not tackled for several decades – how to influence patterns of industrial activity. Nature conservation would be given more emphasis within the planning system as land would have to be found for enhancing ecosystems through afforestation and more nature reserves. Adaptation to climate change would also be a priority.[10]

To achieve an element of de-growth will require a greater attention to low-value activities within market processes and a greater focus on exchange and other activities occurring outside of market processes. So the planning system will need to spend less time engaging with the market actors driving forward urban development and more time engaging with those in the third sector, community groups and voluntary organisations. And within the economic sector, it will need to consider local and small-scale commercial actors more. It will need to foster community activity and schemes that provide for lower-income groups. This could encompass local food-growing schemes, provision for low-value retail facilities and small and medium-sized enterprises (SMEs). Community-based organisations could also underpin the work involved in ecosystem enhancement. There is overlap here with community-based urban regeneration, discussed in Chapter Four.

Rather than looking to build higher land values, planning would positively seek to provide for low-value uses, at least in some locations. Gentrification would not be an indicator of effective planning; rather, the use of land to provide low-cost facilities would be preferred. The indicators of planning would instead look to the well-being and health of all groups in society. Paid employment would not necessarily be favoured over volunteer activism. And indicators of the health of local ecosystems would also feature on a par with these revised welfare indicators.

This would be a huge paradigm shift in what planning has been trying to do. It is proposed in the expectation that reliance on high levels of economic growth may be an inadequate basis for delivering sustainability. Leverage planning will probably never completely disappear; indeed it may be the dominant mode of planning in certain parts of the country where economic growth is present and concentrated. But there is a case to be made for planning using its powers of strategic planning, regulation, land ownership and subsidy to incorporate an element of planning for de-growth as well.

What would be the role of community and stakeholder engagement in such planning for a sustainable future? One of the key features of sustainable development as a goal is that it encompasses the multiple dimensions of economic activity, social well-being and environmental protection. As debates within the literature over the last two decades have testified, there is nothing inherent in the concept that says what level of economic activity, social well-being and environmental protection should be aimed for.

Taking the environmental dimension first, the agenda that arises from a sustainability perspective is fairly clear. The aim is to reduce levels of pollution to air, water and the soil, to reduce resource use and therefore also to reduce waste generation. Preserving valued landscapes and habitats is also a goal. In terms of climate change in particular, the aim is to reduce carbon emissions and to ensure localities are resilient in the face of climate change impacts such as heat waves, periods of heavy rainfall, drought periods, change in soil moisture, sea level rise and coastal erosion.

But how far should planning go in relation to these different environmental goals? There are strong arguments arising from climate science to suggest that where we know how large a reduction in carbon emissions we need to make, we just need to find ways of cascading this down to regional and local levels of the planning system. But in other environmental areas there are questions to be answered. Is any reduction in waste generation sufficient or is the aim to push this right down to near-zero levels? How far do we go in increasing resource efficiencies, say of minerals or water? Should all habitats be protected or can some be developed? And so on....

Turning to the social dimension of sustainability, the agenda here encompasses the provision of employment opportunities to all, the supply of housing of a good quality and at a price that is affordable for all and the creation of a society (as experienced within local areas) that provides security and safety for all. But again there is the issue of how much homelessness or inadequate housing should be tolerated? What level of crime and social anomie? No society expects to eliminate these completely and experience suggests that societies are willing to accept quite high levels. Why else would the London Child Poverty Commission be able to report that over 40% of London's children are living in poverty?[11]

Economists have argued that the solution to this is to evaluate the costs of planning measures as compared with the environmental or social benefits that would result.[12] This would involve quantifying in monetary terms the benefits of environmental protection and social welfare. This approach has long been advocated by environmental economists, and such valuations underpin the influential Stern Review with its argument for taking action on climate change.[13] Within welfare economics, cost benefit analysis has been promoted and used within governmental circles for over half a century.

However, there have been doubts expressed about the values generated by such valuation techniques.[14] Some doubts are practical, for example over the costs of undertaking such valuations on a regular basis to support planning policy in a multitude of localities. Others relate to the methodologies involved and the number of assumptions that are implicit in any valuation exercise. And yet others are more fundamental and concern the model of human valuation involved and whether such an exercise can ever really capture the way that society values different dimensions of sustainable development.

Rather than follow this expert-led approach, critiques of economic valuation approaches go back to the importance of processes of community and stakeholder engagement. Here these are being used not to generate a general view of how sustainable urban change might be understood or a general vision of the future for a locality, but rather to concentrate on the key issues of the level of environmental protection and social welfare that is considered desirable and the way that trade-offs between outcomes within the environmental or social category should be handled. The question is how to engage people in such participatory exercises given the constraints of the collective action problem. Planners need to consider this conundrum if the levels of environmental protection and social well-being are to reflect societal values.

Trading off environmental with social benefits (or vice versa) is trickier. This runs the danger of breaching environmental limits by accepting some social benefits in compensation for environmental change or ignoring the social impacts of environmental protection. One way out of this problem is to focus explicitly on the important issue of who is being affected by the decisions on sustainable outcomes. For experience shows that it is often the most vulnerable groups in society that suffer the most not only from economic deprivation but also from environmental harm. The environmental justice movement has drawn attention to this fact and demanded forms of planning that ensure outcomes that are environmentally sustainable but also socially just (see Chapter Six). Thus public engagement changes by paying particular attention to these vulnerable communities because then it is more likely that environmentally just outcomes will result. This is an argument for public engagement that prioritises poorer groups in society rather than seeking to balance all interests and stakeholders, a balance that often favours the wealthier and those with economic resources to invest.

It is important to recognise that committing resources to such community engagement does not mean that all parties will be happy with the outcome. If private interests have been constrained or a cost imposed on such interests in the pursuit of environmental protection, then it is unreasonable not to expect that party to complain. Furthermore, if environmental injustice is to be tackled, then it is likely that some kind of redistribution will be required and there will be groups that will protest at their loss of amenity, status or resources.

The aim of planning is not to avoid any expression of dissatisfaction with planning outcomes. Rather, there needs to be a degree of confidence that the outcome carries the support of sufficient sectors of society to be legitimate as a position. This goes back to the conflicts between private and collective interests. These conflicts can be handled provided there is a strong and legitimate sense of what the collective interest it. This in part will depend on the transparency, accountability and fairness of the community and stakeholder engagement procedures, as discussed previously. However, this also rests on the extent to which those taking the lead within the planning system – both officers and politicians – are confident that they are delivering urban change that will stand the test of time and that will not be considered a planning failure. This means that planners need to be able to future-proof urban development so that people will continue to view it as a desirable location for living, working and investing in five, 10 or 20 years' time. Such development will also need to fit with the requirements of what may be a radically different kind of economy in the future.

So this means creating urban environments that are not only socially and economically functional but also, given the significance of the climate change agenda, highly resource efficient – ideally not only zero carbon but carbon negative – and resilient in the face of climate change. They should also exhibit greater respect for the contribution of natural spaces and the ecosystems they support. Otherwise the planning system will be engaging in another round of creating less than desirable built environments, even the slums of the future. To achieve these ends, planning needs to develop and use its expertise in creating functional and sustainable urban developments and urban environments.

This means that planning procedures need to find a place for planning expertise. In some approaches (and this has been a criticism of collaborative or deliberative approaches) planning expertise seems to be reduced to knowing how to manage the procedures: how to get more people involved, how to get them to engage fully with the planning issues, and how to ensure the usually silent are given voice. But planning expertise must extend beyond this to provide knowledge about the locality and how it might change, and about how it should change for urban sustainability.[15]

This is not a simple task. Such knowledge is highly contested. So planners will need to choose and prioritise between different bodies of knowledge and the visions that they imply. The planning system has to find ways to handle this by robust questioning of different expertise and knowledge. This will involve specific forums focusing on testing out relevant knowledge claims, particularly on the necessary features of a sustainable urban environment. But planning will also continue to make use of expert agencies such as Natural England or the Environment Agency. The issue is whether the expert agency to support planning for sustainability in terms of climate protection yet exists. And since the challenges of sustainability require planners to choose the appropriate knowledge in highly contested areas, training for planners will need to emphasise the building of critical faculties for assessing sustainability knowledge claims. It is not reasonable to expect planners to be expert in all the facets of a sustainable future, but they need to know where to go for knowledge and how to judge between competing bodies of knowledge.

So perhaps the core competence that a planning system has to develop if it is going to be able to deliver on its vision of a sustainable future is the ability to cope with conflicts: conflicts of interest, of visions of the good life but also of knowledge about what will produce a sustainable future. There is no guarantee that consensus or agreement will result in any of these areas. So planning needs a strong sense of its purpose underpinned by knowledge of what constitutes a sustainable future that remains robust in the face of continuing disagreements. Positioning itself as the mediator between different interests, visions and bodies of knowledge will be insufficient to ensure that sustainable future.

The purpose of planning

So, to conclude briefly, what is the purpose of planning? It is easiest to begin by setting out what the purpose of planning is not. It is not about the planner creating a visionary blueprint for the future on his or her own. It is not about doing planning for others. On the other hand, it is not about big conversations that claim to build national, regional or local consensus but are unable to do so. And it is not about expecting everyone to be interested in and involved in planning debates and decisions. It is not about establishing plans that cannot be implemented and, above all, it is not about ignoring the urgent need for a sustainable path to the future where urban environments are concerned.

So a purposeful planning system should have transparent, accountable and fair means of engaging with communities and stakeholders. There should not be an expectation that everyone will be knocking at the planner's door to get involved but nevertheless it should make a concerted effort to involve a wide range of people and organisations. It should be a system that has robust justifications for involving some more than others, because this is bound to happen;

participatory outcomes should therefore be intentional rather than haphazard. Within this, there should be justified spaces for involving economically and socially vulnerable communities, including spaces to consider the differential impact of climate change and other environmental impacts. The planning system would make selective use of deliberative processes to support decisions, in particular about the scale and kind of local environmental protection and welfare benefits that planning should be seeking to deliver in a sustainable future, that is, to address difficult questions of trade-offs.

Such a planning system would recognise that it is highly dependent on market actors for fulfilling its goals at present and take care to ensure that this dependence does not skew the overall outcomes of planning decisions. It would also recognise the limitations of the tools that planners are able to control, particularly regulatory tools, given this market dependence. It would seek to make full use of the tools at its disposal rather than rely too heavily on regulation. However, the planning system would also be actively considering how to incorporate a dimension that is about planning for de-growth. This may involve moving away from a reliance on property-led local economic development, particularly retail-led growth. It would involve looking to economic activities that occur outside of the market-place or that deliver welfare and employment through low values uses of land.

While accepting that people's current interests and values need to be given expression within the planning system, a purposeful planning system would acknowledge that this will not provide sufficient space to consider how the future may be made sustainable. Current generations do not always speak for future generations. Therefore planners have a responsibility to bring persuasive arguments to planning debates and decision-making forums about the need to consider the sustainability of urban environments and about the means of achieving such sustainability. This responsibility will put particular demands on their ability to negotiate the complicated and contested field of knowledge about sustainability. But without this, a planning system may be judged from the perspective of the next generation to have been wandering aimlessly through the early 21st century.

Notes

one

[1] Howard (1902/1945), p 54.
[2] Rydin (2003a), Chapter 8.
[3] Zola (1883; 2002).
[4] Broadbent (1977), Castells (1979), and Harloe and Lebas (1981) are a sample of such commentators.
[5] Hall (1982) provides a readable review of past planning failures; Jacobs (1961) gives a classic critique of planning outcomes.
[6] See Duncan (1989) on Sweden, and Verhage and Needham (1997) on the Netherlands.
[7] Brindley et al (1996), Chapter 6, and Brownill (1990) provide accounts of the London Docklands experiment.
[8] Hall (2002) provides a historical review of planning that emphasises the role of transport infrastructure; Graham and Marvin (2001) provide a comprehensive and sophisticated take on the interrelationships between urban growth and infrastructure networks.
[9] Graham and Marvin (2001) provides the classic account of this argument.
[10] Allmendinger (1997) gives an account of such zones in the UK during the 1980s and early 1990s.
[11] www.hmrc.gov.uk/ria/9-zero-carbon-homes.pdf
[12] Whitehead (1999) discusses this in the UK context.
[13] Cullingworth (1993) provides a survey on zoning in the US context.
[14] Rydin (2003b) or Cullingworth and Nadin (2006) provide an introduction to the UK system.
[15] Healey et al (1995) is a useful reference to planning gain in the UK context.
[16] Rydin (2010), Chapter 9, reviews such schemes.

two

[1] Rydin (2003b), p 10, provides a summary of such models, followed by further explanation in Chapters 1-4; Allmendinger (2002) provides a full review.
[2] Scott (2003) explores modernism and planning.
[3] Lindblom's account of 'muddling through' (2003) is the classic critique of modernist planning as a process, but see Sabatier (2007) for a defence of a version of this process, known as the stages model. Rydin (2003a), Chapter 5, provides an analysis of why this model is so resistant to critique in practice.
[4] This is a reference to the model of planning deduced from Patrick Geddes' writings; Rubin (2009) provides a recent account.
[5] Barrett and Fudge (1981) is an excellent collection exploring how policy formulation and implementation are intertwined.
[6] Rydin (1986) details this with regard to residential development.
[7] Rhodes (1997) is a classic text on governance; Pierre (2000) is a helpful collection; and in a local context, the two collections edited by Stoker (1999, 2000) are useful.

[8] www.bebirmingham.org.uk/page.php?id=21&mt=t

[9] Birmingham City Council (2008) *Statement of Community Involvement*, S 5.3, available at www.birmingham.gov.uk/cs/Satellite?c=Page&childpagename=Development-Planning%2FPageLayout&cid=1223092558579&pagename=BCC%2FCommon%2FWrapper%2FWrapper

[10] Healey (2000) is the definitive account of collaborative planning.

[11] Oxley (2004) provides a classic economic justification of planning in terms of handling externalities.

[12] Parr (2002) is a paper exploring the concept of agglomeration economies.

[13] A text such as Balchin and Kieve (1982) covers these models.

[14] The 18th report by the Royal Commission on Environmental Pollution (1995) provides a wealth of evidence on this in Chapter 9.

[15] This was a key argument of the Urban Task Force (2005).

[16] The European Spatial Development Perspective or ESDP was produced by the EU Committee on Spatial Development in 1999.

[17] ESDP (1999), s 1.1(7), p 7.

[18] ESDP (1999), s 1.1(8), pp 7-8

[19] CLG (2008), s 2.1, p 4.

[20] RCEP (1995), Chapter 6, provides evidence for this point.

[21] The Transport 2000 report by Steer Davies Gleave (2006) supports this point.

[22] Docherty and Shaw (2008) undertake a thorough exploration of the 'new realism'.

[23] Newman and Kenworthy's analysis (1989) of the relationship between petrol consumption and urban densities on a global and US basis was central in making this new planning orthodoxy on urban densities.

[24] Newman and Kenworthy (1999) discuss all these aspects of planning for sustainable travel.

[25] Rydin (2010) discusses infrastructure for sustainable urban development in Chapters 2 and 8.

[26] The Foresight report (2008) makes this case strongly in the case of energy infrastructure.

[27] A selection of papers on decentralised energy is provided in a special issue of *Energy Policy* (2008).

[28] A discussion of sustainable urban drainage in terms of the 'absorbent city' is given by White (2008).

[29] Ostrom et al (1961), Keohane and Ostrom (1995) and Innes and Brooher (2003) provide different takes on this issue.

[30] The Conservative Party (2010) includes this and other suggestions for reform of the planning system.

three

[1] Population Division of the Department of Economic and Social Affairs of the United Nations Secretariat, *World Population Prospects: The 2008 Revision*, http://esa.un.org/unpp

[2] Long-Term International Migration (LTIM), International Passenger Survey (IPS), Office for National Statistics.

[3] NHSCR Inter-regional migration movements, within the UK during the year ending September 2006, Office for National Statistics.

[4] Censuses, Labour Force Survey, Office for National Statistics; Censuses, General Register Office for Scotland; Household estimates, Communities and Local Government; Household estimates, Scottish Executive.

[5] www.communities.gov.uk/housing/housingmanagementcare/emptyhomes/

[6] English House Condition Survey 2007, Department of Communities and Local Government, 2009.

[7] Murdoch and Abram (2002) give a very interesting analysis of this issue.

[8] Evans (1991) is a classic argument of this kind; Cheshire and Sheppard (2005) is another example of a proposal deriving from this economic perspective.

[9] The influential Barker Report (2004) expounded this view.

[10] An excellent account of the credit crunch is Krugman (2009).

[11] This was in the Housing Green Paper of 2007, issued by the Department of Communities and Local Government (see CLG, 2007).

[12] Reported on http://news.bbc.co.uk/1/hi/uk_politics/8600961.stm

[13] Hebbert (1992) reviews the New Towns programme; a further account can be found in Chapters 5-8 of Ward (2004).

[14] www.communities.gov.uk/housing/housingsupply/ecotowns/

[15] www.arup.com/_assets/_download/8CFDEE1A-CC3E-EA1A-25FD80B2315B50FD.pdf

[16] See Hall (2002).

[17] Hall et al (1973) is the classic study on this.

[18] Elson (1986) provides the definitive history of the green belt concept.

[19] Walton (2000) provides support for this point.

[20] Forrest and Murie (1988) document this period in housing policy.

[21] www.communities.gov.uk/publications/housing/housingengland2006-07

[22] Burgess et al (2007) and Crook and Whitehead (2002) explore the application of this policy.

four

[1] A text such as Balchin and Kieve (1982) will provide an economic explanation of such market processes.

[2] Gibbons and Machin (2003) is an empirical analysis of this relationship.

[3] Conservative Party policy (2010) was to offer additional taxation revenue to local councils in return for building more affordable housing, which is an interesting take on this interrelationship between urban development and local government finance.

[4] Rex and Moore (1969) is the classic study on this topic but there is a huge literature documenting space and race across the city

[5] Turok (1992), Healey (1992) and Imrie and Thomas (1993) provide some references on this approach.

[6] See Hall (1982) for some examples.

[7] Franck (1984) attempts to resurrect this controversial term.

[8] Young and Willmott (1986) remains the classic reference for this point.

[9] There is a useful special issue of *Urban Studies* (2001) on the neighbourhood, which includes papers on social capital and its significance in defining local community.

[10] Smith and Williams (1986) and Smith (1996) provide good accounts of gentrification. Punter (2010) provides plenty of evidence of this across a range of British cities.

[11] Coaffee and Healey (2003) provide a case study of recent attempts at community engagement in Newcastle.

[12] Lawless (1994), Lowndes et al (1997) and Carley et al (2002) document the partnership approach in urban regeneration. Hastings (1996) and Atkinson (1999) unpack the concept.

[13] Brindley et al (1996) introduces the concept of leverage planning.

[14] See the Milton Keynes Partnership website at www.miltonkeynespartnership. info/about_MKP/business_plans_infrastructure_tariff.php

[15] See www.southwark.gov.uk/section106

[16] See Seyfang (2004) on time banks, Schmelzkopf (1995) on community gardening and Edgcomb et al (1996) on micro-credit, all in England or US context. References on developing country contexts include Carley et al (2001). Shaftoe and Tallon (2010) also document some interesting initiatives in the inner city in Bristol.

[17] Ostrom (1990) is the classic reference here, but see also Maida (2007).

[18] CLG Housing Statistics, Table 111 Conversions and demolitions: estimated annual gains and losses, England, from 1991/92; see also Boardman (2007).

[19] www.communities.gov.uk/housing/housingsupply/housingmarketrenewal/

[20] www.creationtrust.org/index.php?miid=1974

[21] Boardman et al (2005) provide the pioneering analysis of this topic.

[22] Power (2008) provides a vigorous rebuttal of the case for demolition.

[23] Power (2008), p 4488.

five

[1] In his paper, Sønderskov (2008) reports these membership level within a cross-national study. See also Lowe and Goyder (1983) for a study of environmental groups in the UK.

[2] Data are taken from Hicks and Allen (1999)

[3] Macnaghten and Urry (1998) and Short (1991) detail this.

[4] Shucksmith (1990) details these issues.

[5] The New Economics Foundation (2005) coined the phrase 'clone town'.

[6] Sources for these figures are: www.english-heritage.org.uk, www.defra.gov.uk, www.wetlands.org and http://whc.unesco.org/

[7] See Macnaghten and Urry (1998), Chapter 6.

[8] See, for example, the work of the Equiano Centre (www.ucl.ac.uk/equianocentre/) on the African diaspora in Britain.

[9] Environmental anthropology has played a role in this change; see Milton (1993, 1996).

[10] Lowe and Goyder (1983) confirms this.

[11] Larkham (1996) is a useful reference on conservation of the built environment; see also Larkham and Jones (1993).

[12] But see the work of Space Syntax, which seeks to map and understand how people use space with a view to better planning of urban areas (www.spacesyntax.org/).

[13] Commission on Architecture and the Built Environment (www.cabe.org.uk) have developed a range of resources to underpin such place-making activity.

[14] Details of the Low Energy Victorian House can be found at www.levh.org.uk/

[15] Pointer (2005) provides this data.

[16] Pepper (1996) is a good introduction to the concept of transcendentalism. A variety of eco-culture texts, all in a US context, provide an exploration of its impact in more depth: Cantrill and Oravec (1996), Part 1; Muir and Veenendall (1996), Part 3; and Herndl and Brown (1996). Macnaghten and Urry (1998) touch on this in a UK context.

[17] For more details see www.mosaicnationalparks.org/About_Mosaic/
[18] This is recognised by the UN Environment Programme Global Partnership on Cities and Biodiversity (www.unep.org/urban_environment/issues/biodiversity.asp)
[19] But see Winter (2000) and Primdahl et al (2003) for analysis of the impact of these reforms.
[20] Senecah (1996) is an interesting case study based in the Adirondacks, US.
[21] See Edwards (2010) for an assessment of this regeneration scheme.
[22] See Shucksmith (1990) on this.
[23] Most conservation references detail this effect but see also Zukin (1989) for the New York case.

six

[1] Wykes (2000) provides a media-oriented analysis of such cases.
[2] This is documented in Rydin and Pennington (2000); see also Pennington and Rydin (2001) for the role of the local media in such protests.
[3] The Sustainable Communities Plan (*Sustainable Communities: Building for the Future*) was launched in 2003: available at www.communities.gov.uk/communities/sustainablecommunities/sustainablecommunities/
[4] The website for the local oppositional group, Hacan Clear Skies, is www.hacan.org.uk/index.php. The Labour government supported the proposal for a further runway at Heathrow, but it was opposed by the Conservative Party while in opposition.
[5] This is discussed in the Foresight (2008) report on sustainable energy management and the built environment.
[6] The consultation draft of the National Policy Statement for Nuclear Power Generation, issued in November 2009, sets this policy out.
[7] The history of nuclear public inquiries has been documented in Kemp (1985) and O'Riordan et al (1988).
[8] The Infrastructure Planning Commission's website is http://infrastructure.independent.gov.uk/
[9] See Davoudi and Evans (2005), Davoudi (2006) and Tunesi (2010) for discussion of waste planning.
[10] The classic reference for the concept of sustainable development is WCED (1987), also known as the Brundtland Report.
[11] But see the arguments in Jackson (2010), which are discussed further in Chapter Eight.
[12] Neumayer (2003) provides a good review of these arguments.
[13] There is a wide literature on environmental justice including Agyeman (2005) and *Geoforum* (2006).
[14] This story is well told in Harvey (1996), Chapter 13.
[15] The key reference here is Olsen (1971).
[16] A range of references on these approaches include Owens (2000), Bloomfield et al (2001), Beierle and Konisky (2001), Petts (2001) and Ward et al (2003).
[17] The Conservative Party was proposing (prior to the general election in 2010) to promote mayors in major urban conurbations. Stoker (2007) discusses mayors in the UK context from the experience in the US.
[18] This is a difficult area to research but Saunders (1979) undertook this in the 1970s.
[19] Updated guidance on this has been published by the Local Government Association (2009).

seven

[1] Ceiraad (1999) is a collection of anthropological perspectives on the home. Miller (2009) is another anthropological approach, this time to things within the home.
[2] Merrett (1982) explores all the implications of high rates of owner-occupation in Britain.
[3] The website for the Oxford shark is www.headington.org.uk/shark/
[4] Up-to-date details of the requirements for obtaining planning permission for domestic extensions are available on the Planning Portal at www.planningportal.gov.uk
[5] This is from CLG's Development Control Statistics for England, available at: www.communities.gov.uk/publications/corporate/statistics/developmentcontrol200809
[6] Householder Development Consents Review Key Facts available at www.communities.gov.uk/planningandbuilding/planning/planningpolicyimplementation/reformplanningsystem/householderdevelopmentconsents/keyfacts/
[7] The relevant section of the Planning Inspectorate website is www.planning-inspectorate.gov.uk/pins/appeals/householder_appeals.htm
[8] Chung (1994) and Webster (1998) expound this approach.
[9] Forester (1987) provides a view of mediation in planning from a US perspective; CLG (2006) reports on a trial exercise using mediation in the UK planning system.
[10] A classic reference on social capital is Putnam (2001).
[11] Carmona et al (2003) is a good guide to the role of urban design.
[12] A point also stressed in Newman and Kenworthy (1999).
[13] Leyden (2003) reports one example of this research.
[14] The *woonerf* concept is discussed in Ben-Joseph (1995), considering its application in the US suburban context.
[15] Williams (2005) reports research supporting this claim.
[16] Foresight (2008) provides this information.
[17] The Code for Sustainable Homes can be found at www.communities.gov.uk/planningandbuilding/buildingregulations/legislation/codesustainable/
[18.] Chapters 6 and 9 of Rydin (2010) discuss regulation, the Merton Rule and the definition of zero carbon in relation to producing more sustainable housing and urban development.
[19] Full details of the CLG policy for delivering zero-carbon housebuilding by 2016 are available at www.communities.gov.uk/planningandbuilding/theenvironment/zerocarbonhomes/
[20] Foresight (2008) discusses retrofitting the existing stock in some detail.
[21] Originally the Bill which led to the Sustainable and Secure Buildings Act 2004 was intended to incorporate this provision.
[22] The website for the Marburg initiative is available at www.marburg.de/detail/73351 and for the Barcelona ordinance at www.barcelonaenergia.cat/eng/operations/ost.htm
[23] Foresight (2008) reports this.
[24] Mitchell et al (2006) investigates such tariffs.
[25] Hinnells (2008) reviews the potential of CHP and associated district heating.
[26] Again Foresight (2008) reviews these arguments.

eight

[1] Healey (2000), Hillier (2003), Innes (2004) and Sandercock (1998) are the key references.

[2] Sandercock (1998) argues this strongly.

[3] Evans (1991) is an example of this approach.

[4] This is one of the hopes of the spatial planning approach.

[5] Key documents are the UK government's Sustainable Development Strategy (HM Government, 2005) and the UK Low Carbon Transition Plan (HM Government, 2009). Planning is specifically guided by Planning Policy Statement 1 (CLG, 2005); see also the consultation draft of a Planning Policy Statement on planning for a low carbon future in a changing climate (CLG, 2010) – both PPSs are issued by the Department for Communities and Local Government (CLG). In addition, the Planning and Compulsory Purchase Act 2004 requires all planning to be exercised 'with the objective of contributing to the achievement of sustainable development' (s 39). The Climate Change Act 2008 sets binding carbon emissions targets which will impact on planning practice.

[6] See Gouldson and Murphy (1998, 2002) for a useful account of ecological modernisation.

[7] The following figures are all taken from Jackson (2010), p 12.

[8] Jackson (2010), p 128.

[9] Jackson (2010), p 130.

[10] See Davoudi et al (2009) for accounts of how planning can provide for climate change adaptation alongside mitigation strategies.

[11] See the London Child Poverty Commission website at http://213.86.122.139/

[12] Relevant texts expounding this approach are Pearce (1990) and Turner et al (1994).

[13] Stern (2007) was a report commissioned by HM Treasury.

[14] Foster (1997) is an excellent collection of papers critiquing the neoclassical economic perspective on valuing the environment.

[15] This argument is developed at greater length in Rydin (2007).

References

Agyeman, J. (2005) *Sustainable communities and the challenge of environmental justice*, New York, NY: New York University Press.

Allmendinger, P. (1997) *Thatcherism and planning: the case of simplified planning zones*, Aldershot, Hants: Ashgate.

Allmendinger, P. (2002) *Planning theory* Basingstoke, Hants: Palgrave.

Atkinson, R. (1999) 'Discourses of partnership and empowerment in contemporary British urban regeneration', *Urban Studies*, vol 36, no 1, pp 59-72.

Balchin, P. and Kieve, J. (1982) *Urban land economics*, Basingstoke, Hants: Macmillan.

Barker, K. (2004) *Delivering stability: securing our future housing needs, Barker review of housing supply – final report*, London: HM Treasury.

Barrett, S. and Fudge, C. (1981) *Policy and action: essays on the implementation of public policy*, London: Methuen.

Beierle, T. and Konisky, D. (2001) 'What are we gaining from stakeholder involvement? Observations from environmental planning in the Great Lakes', *Environment and Planning C*, vol 19, pp 515-27.

Ben-Joseph, E. (1995) 'Changing the residential street scene: adapting the shared street (woonerf) concept to the suburban environment', *Journal of the American Planning Association*, vol 61, no 4, pp 504-15.

Bloomfield, D., Collins, K., Fry, C. and Munton, R. (2001) 'Deliberation and inclusion: vehicles for increasing trust in UK public governance?', *Environment and Planning C*, vol 19, pp 501-13.

Boardman, B. (2007) 'Examining the carbon agenda via the *40% House* scenario', *Building Research and Information*, vol 35, no 4, pp 363-78.

Boardman, B., Darby, S., Killip, G., Hinnels, M., Jardine, C., Palmer, J. and Sinden, G. (2005) *40% House*, Oxford: Environmental Change Institute, University of Oxford.

Brindley, T., Rydin, Y. and Stoker, G. (1996) *Remaking planning: the politics of urban change*, London: Routledge.

Broadbent (1977), *Planning and profit in the urban economy*, London: Routledge.

Brownill, S. (1990) *Developing London's docklands: another great planning disaster?,* London: Paul Chapman Publishing Ltd.

Burgess, G., Monk, S. and Whitehead, C. (2007) *The provision of affordable housing through section 106: the situation in 2007,* RICS Research Paper Series, London: RICS.

Cantrill, J.G. and Oravec, C.L. (1996) *The symbolic earth*, Lexington, KY: University Press of Kentucky.

Carley, M., Chapman, M., Kirk, K., Hastings, A. and Young, R. (2002) *Urban regeneration through partnership: a study in nine regions in England, Scotland and Wales*, Bristol: The Policy Press for Joseph Rowntree Foundation.

Carley, M., Jenkins, P. and Smith, H. (2001) *Urban development and civil society*, London: Earthscan.

Carmona, M., Heath, T., Tiesdell, S. and Oc, T. (2003) *Public places – urban spaces: the dimensions of urban design* Oxford: Architectural Press.

Castells (1979), *The urban question: a Marxist approach*, translated by Alan Sheridan, London: Edward Arnold.

Ceiraad, I. (1999) *At Home: an anthropology of domestic space*, New York, NY: Syracuse University Press.

Cheshire, P. and Sheppard, S. (2005) 'The introduction of price signals into land use planning decision-making: a proposal', *Urban Studies,* vol 42, no 4, pp 647-63.

Chung, L.L.W. (1994) 'The economics of land-use zoning: a literature review and analysis of the work of Coase', *Town Planning Review,* vol 65, no 1, pp 77-98.

CLG (Department for Communities and Local Government) (2005) *Planning Policy Statement 1: delivering sustainable development*, London: CLG.

CLG (2006) *Mediation in the planning system*, London: CLG.

CLG (2007) *Homes for the future: more affordable, more sustainable* (the housing green paper), London: CLG.

CLG (2008) *Planning Policy Statement 12: creating strong safe and prosperous communities through local spatial planning*, London: CLG

CLG (2010) *Consultation on a planning policy statement: planning for a low carbon future in a changing climate*, London: CLG.

Coaffee, J. and Healey, P. (2003) '"My voice: my place": tracking transformations in urban governance', *Urban Studies*, vol 40, no 10, pp 1979-99.

Conservative Party (2010) *Open source planning*, Policy Green Paper No 14, London: The Conservative Party.

Crook, T. and Whitehead, C. (2002) 'Social housing and planning gain: is this an appropriate way of providing affordable housing?' *Environment and Planning A*, vol 34, no 7, pp. 1259-79.

Cullingworth, J.B. (1993) *The political culture of planning: American land use planning in comparative perspective*, London: Routledge.

Cullingworth, J.B. and Nadin, V. (2006) *Town and country planning in the UK,* 14th edn, London: Routledge.

Davoudi, S. (2006) 'The evidence-policy interface in strategic waste planning for urban environments: the "technical" and the "social" dimensions', *Environment and Planning C*, vol 24, pp 681-700.

Davoudi, S. and Evans, N. (2005) 'The challenge of governance in regional waste planning', *Environment and Planning C*, vol 23, pp 493-517.

Davoudi, S., Crawford, J., and Mehmood, A. (2009) *Planning for climate change: strategies for mitigation and adaptation for spatial planners*, London: Earthscan.

Docherty, I. and Shaw, J. (2008) *Traffic jam: ten years of 'sustainable' transport in the UK*, Bristol: Policy Press.

Duncan, S. (1989) 'Development gains and housing provision in Britain and Sweden', *Transactions of the Institute of British Geographers*, New Series, vol 14, no 2, pp 157-172.

Edgcomb, E., Klein, J. and Clark, P. (1996) *The practice of microenterprise in the US: strategies, costs and effectiveness*, The Self-Employment Learning Project, Queenstown, MD: The Aspen Institute.

Edwards, M. (2010) 'King's Cross: renaissance for whom?' in J. Punter (ed) *Urban design and the British urban renaissance*, London: Routledge, pp 189-205.

Elson, M. (1986) *Green belts: conflict mediation in the urban fringe*, London: Butterworth-Heinemann.

Energy Policy (2008) Special Issue on Foresight, Sustainable Energy Management and the Built Environment Project, vol 36, no 12.

ESDP (1999) *European Spatial Development Perspective: towards balanced and sustainable development of the territory of the European Union (ESPD)*, European Committee on Spatial Development, Brussels: European Commission.

Evans, A. W. (1991) '"Rabbit Hutches on Postage Stamps": planning, development and political economy', *Urban Studies*, vol 28, no 6, pp 853-70.

Foresight (2008) *Powering our lives: sustainable energy management in the built environment*, London: Government Office for Science.

Forester, J. (1987) 'Planning in the face of conflict: negotiation and mediation strategies in local land use regulation', *Journal of the American Planning Association*, vol 53, no 3, pp 303-14.

Forrest, R. and Murie, A. (1988) *Selling the welfare state: the privatization of public housing*, London: Routledge.

Foster, J. (ed) (1997) *Valuing nature: economics, ethics and environment*, London: Routledge.

Franck, K. (1984) 'Exorcising the ghost of physical determinism', *Environment and Behavior*, vol 16, no 4, pp 411-35.

Geoforum (2006) Special Issue on Environmental Justice, vol 37, no 5.

Gibbons, S. and Machin, S. (2003) 'Valuing English primary schools', *Journal of Urban Economics*, vol 53, no 2, pp 197-219.

Gouldson, A and Murphy, J. (1998) *Regulatory realities*, London: Earthscan.

Gouldson, A and Murphy, J. (2002) 'Ecological modernisation: restructuring industrial economies', *Political Quarterly*, vol 68, no B, pp 74-86.

Graham, S. and Marvin, S. (2001) *Splintering urbanism: networked infrastructures, technological mobilities and the urban condition*, London: Routledge.

Hall (1982) *Great planning disasters*, California, CA: University of Berkeley Press.

Hall, P. (2002) *Urban and regional planning*, 4th edn, London: Penguin Books.

Hall, P., Graley, H., Drewett, R. and Thomas, R. (1973) *Containment of urban England ,* London: Allen & Unwin.

Harloe, M. and Lebas, E. (eds) (1981) *City, class and capital: new developments in the political economy of cities and regions*, London: Edward Arnold.

Harvey, D. (1996) *Justice, nature and the geography of difference*, Oxford: Blackwell.

Hastings, A. (1996) 'Unravelling the process of "partnership" in urban regeneration policy', *Urban Studies*, vol 33, no 2, pp 253-68.

Healey, P. (1992) *Rebuilding the city: property-led urban regeneration*, London: Chapman & Hall.

Healey, P. (2000) *Collaborative planning: shaping places in fragmented societies*, London: Palgrave.

Healey, P., Purdue, M. and Ennis, F. (1995) *Negotiating development: rationales and practice for development obligations,* London: E&FN Spon.

Hebbert, M. (1992) 'The British garden city: metamorphosis', in S. Ward (ed) *The garden city: past, present, and future*, London: E & FN Spon, pp 165-186.

Herndl, C.G. and Brown, S.C. (1996) *Green culture: environmental rhetoric in contemporary America*, Madison, WI: University of Wisconsin Press.

Hicks, J. and Allen, G. (1999) *A century of change: trends in UK statistics since 1900*, Research Paper 99/111, Social and General Statistics Section, London: House of Commons Library.

Hillier, J. (2003) `Agonizing over consensus: why Habermasian ideals cannot be "real"', *Planning Theory*, vol 2, no 1, pp 37-59.

Hinnells, M. (2008) 'Combined heat and power in industry and buildings', *Energy Policy*, vol 36, no 12, pp 4522-26.

HM Government (2005) *National sustainable development strategy: securing the future*, Cm 6467, London: HMSO.

HM Government (2009) *UK low carbon transition plan: national strategy for climate and energy*, London: HMSO.

Howard, E. (1902/1945) *Garden cities of tomorrow*, 1960 reprint, London: Faber and Faber.

Imrie, R. and Thomas, H. (1993) 'The limits of property led regeneration', *Environment and Planning C*, vol 11, pp 87-102.

Innes, J. (2004) 'Consensus building: clarification for the critics', *Planning Theory*, vol 3, no 1, pp 5-20.

———

Innes, J. and Brooher, D. (2003) 'Collaborative policy making: governance through dialogue', in M. Hajer. and H. Wagenaar (eds) *Deliberative policy analysis: understanding governance in the network society*, Cambridge: Cambridge University Press, pp 33-59.

Jackson, T. (2010) *Prosperity without growth*, London: Earthscan.

Jacobs, J. (1961) *The death and life of great American cities*, New York, NY: Random House.

Kemp, R. (1985) 'Planning, public hearings and the politics of discourse', in J. Forester (ed.) *Critical theory and public life*, Cambridge, MA: MIT Press, pp 177-201.

Keohane, R. and Ostrom, E. (1995) *Local commons and global interdependence*, London: Sage Publications.

Krugman, P. (2009) *The return of depression economics and the crisis of 2008*, London: Penguin Books.

Larkham, P. (1996) *Conservation and the city*, London: Routledge.

Larkham, P. and Jones, A. (1993) 'Conservation and conservation areas in the UK: a growing problem', *Planning, Practice and Research*, vol 8, no 2, pp 19-29.

Lawless, P. (1994) 'Partnership in urban regeneration in the UK: the Sheffield Central Area Study', *Urban Studies*, vol 31, no 8, pp 1303-24.

Leyden, K. (2003) 'Social capital and the built environment: the importance of walkable neighbourhoods', *American Journal of Public Health*, vol 93, pp 1546-51.

Lindblom, C.E. (2003) 'The science of "muddling through"', in S. Campbell and S. Fainstein (eds) *Readings in Planning Theory*, 2nd edn, Cambridge, MA: Blackwell, pp 196-209.

Local Government Association (2009) *Probity in planning: the role of councillors* London: LGA

Lowe, P. and Goyder, J. (1983) *Environmental groups in politics*, London: George Allen and Unwin.

Lowndes, V., Nanton, P., McCabe, A. and Skelcher, C. (1997) 'Networks, partnerships and urban regeneration', *Local Economy*, vol 11, no 4, pp 333-42.

Macnaghten, P. and Urry, J. (1998) *Contested natures*, London: Sage.

Maida, C.A. (ed) (2007) *Sustainability and communities of place*, Oxford: Bergham Books.

Merrett, S. (1982) *Owner occupation in Britain*, London: RKP.

Miller, D. (2009) *The comfort of things,* Cambridge: Polity Press.

Milton, K. (ed) (1993) *Environmentalism: the view from anthropology*, London: Routledge.

Milton, K. (1999) *Environmentalism and cultural theory: exploring the role of anthropology in environmental discourse*, London: Routledge.

Mitchell, C., Bauknecht, D. and Connor, P.M. (2006) 'Effectiveness through risk reduction: a comparison of the renewable obligation in England and Wales and the feed-in system in Germany', *Energy Policy*, vol 34, no 3, pp 297-305.

Muir, S.A. and Veenendall, T.L. (eds) (1996) *Earthtalk: communication empowerment for environmental action*, Westport, CT: Praeger.

Murdoch, J. and Abram, S. (2002) *Rationalities of planning: development versus environment in planning for housing*, Aldershot, Hants: Ashgate.

Neumayer, E. (2003) *Weak versus strong sustainability: exploring the limits of two opposing paradigms*, Cheltenham: Edward Elgar.

New Economics Foundation (2005) *Clone town Britain: the survey results on the bland state of the nation*, London: NEF.

Newman, P. and Kenworthy, J. (1989) 'Gasoline consumption and cities: a comparison of U.S. cities with a global survey', *Journal of the American Planning Association*, vol 55, no 1, pp 24-37.

Newman, P. and Kenworthy, J. (1999) *Sustainability and cities: overcoming automobile dependence*, Washington, DC: Island Press.

O'Riordan, T., Kemp, R. and Purdue, M. (1988) *Sizewell B: an anatomy of the inquiry*, London: Macmillan.

Olsen, M. (1971) *The logic of collective action: public goods and the theory of groups*, Harvard Economic Studies Volume CXXIV, Department of Economics, Cambridge, MA: Harvard University.

Ostrom. E. (1990) *Governing the commons: the evolution of institutions for collective action*, Cambridge: University of Cambridge.

Ostrom, V., Tiebout, C. and Warren, R. (1961) 'The organization of government in metropolitan areas: a theoretical inquiry', *The American Political Science Review*, vol 55, no 4. pp 831-42.

Owens, S. (2000) 'Commentary: "engaging the public": information and deliberation in environmental policy', *Environment and Planning A*, vol 32, pp 1141-48.

Oxley, M. (2004) *Economics, planning and housing*, London: Palgrave.

Parr, J.B. (2002) 'Agglomeration economies: ambiguities and confusions', *Environment and Planning A*, vol 34, pp 717-31.

Pearce, D. (1990) *Economics of natural resources and the environment*, London: Harvester Wheatsheaf.

Pennington, M. and Rydin, Y. (2001) 'Discourses of the prisoners' dilemma: the role of the local press in environmental policy', *Environmental Politics*, vol 10, no 3, pp 48-71.

Pepper, D. (1996) *Modern environmentalism: an introduction*, London: Routledge.

Petts, J. (2001) 'Evaluating the effectiveness of deliberative processes: waste management case studies', *Journal of Environmental Planning and Management*, vol 44, no 2, pp 207-26.

Pierre, J. (ed) (2000) *Debating governance: authority, steering and democracy*, Oxford: OUP.

Pointer, G. (2005) *Focus on people and migration, Chapter 3 – The UK's major urban areas*, UK National Statistics, London: NSO, available from www.statistics.gov.uk/downloads/theme_compendia/fom2005/03_FOPM_UrbanAreas.pdf

Power, A. (2008) 'Does demolition or refurbishment of old and inefficient homes help to increase our environmental, social and economic viability?', *Energy Policy*, vol 36, no 12, pp 4487-501.

Primdahl, J., Peco, B., Schramek, J., Andersen, E. and Onate, J.J. (2003) 'Environmental effects of agri-environmental schemes in Western Europe', *Journal of Environmental Management*, vol 67, no 2, pp 129-38.

Punter, J. (ed) (2010) *Urban design and the British urban renaissance*, London: Routledge.

Putnam, R.D. (2001) *Bowling alone: the collapse and revival of American community*, New York, NY: Simon and Schuster.

RCEP (Royal Commission on Environmental Pollution) (1995) *Transport and the environment*, Oxford: OUP.

Rex, J. and Moore, R.S. (1969) *Race, community and conflict: a study of Sparkbrook*, Oxford: Oxford University Press for the Institute of Race Relations.

Rhodes, R.A.W. (1997) *Understanding governance*, Milton Keynes: Open University Press.

Rubin, N. (2009) 'The changing appreciation of Patrick Geddes: a case study in planning history', *Planning Perspectives,* vol 24, no 3, pp 349-66.

Rydin, Y. (1986) *Housing land policy*, Aldershot: Gower.

Rydin, Y. (2003a) *Conflict, consensus and rationality in environmental planning: an institutional discourse approach*, Oxford: OUP.

Rydin, Y. (2003b) *Urban and environmental planning in the UK*, 2nd edn, London: Palgrave.

Rydin, Y. (2007) 'Re-examining the role of knowledge within planning theory', *Planning Theory*, vol 6, pp 52-68.

Rydin, Y. (2010) *Governing for sustainable urban development*, London: Earthscan.

Rydin, Y. and Pennington, M. (2000) 'Researching social capital in local environmental policy contexts', *Policy and Politics*, vol 28, no 2, pp 33-49.

Sabatier, P. (2007) *Theories of the policy process,* Boulder, CO: Westview Press.

Sandercock, L. (1998) *Towards Cosmopolis: planning for multicultural cities*, Chichester: J. Wiley.

Saunders, P. (1979) *Urban politics: a sociological interpretation*, London: Hutchinson.

Schmelzkopf, K. (1995) 'Urban community gardens as contested space', *Geographical Review,* vol 85, no 3, pp 364-81.

Scott, J.C. (2003) 'Authoritarian high modernism', in S. Campbell and S. Fainstein (eds) *Readings in Planning Theory*, 2nd edn, Cambridge, MA: Blackwell, pp. 125-41.

Senecah, S. (1996) 'Forever wild or forever in battle: metaphors of empowerment in the continuing controversy over the Adirondacks', in S.A. Muir and T.L. Veenendall (eds) *Earthtalk: communication empowerment for environmental action*, Westport, CT: Praeger, pp 95-118.

Seyfang, G. (2004) 'Time banks: rewarding community self-help in the inner city?' *Community Development Journal*, vol 39, pp 62-71.

Shaftoe, H. and Tallon, A. (2010) 'Bristol: not a design-led urban renaissance', in J. Punter (ed) *Urban design and the British urban renaissance*, London: Routledge, pp 115-31.

Short, J.R. (1991) *Imagined country*, London: Routledge.

Shucksmith, M. (1990) *Housebuilding in Britain's countryside*, London: Routledge.

Smith, N. (1996) *The new urban frontier: gentrification and the revanchist city*, London: Routledge.

Smith, N. and Williams, P. (1986) *Gentrification of the city*, London: Allen & Unwin.

Sønderskov, K.M. (2008) 'Environmental group membership, collective action and generalised trust', *Environmental Politics*, vol 17, no 1, pp 78-94.

Steer Davies Gleave (2006) *Driving up carbon dioxide emissions from transport: an analysis of current government projects*, London: Transport 2000.

Stern, N. (2007) *The economics of climate change: the Stern Review*, Cambridge: Cambridge University Press.

Stoker, G. (1999) *The new management of British local governance*, London: Macmillan.

Stoker, G. (2000) *The new politics of British local governance*, London: Macmillan.

Stoker, G. (2007) 'Drawing lessons from US experience: an elected mayor for British local government', *Public Administration*, vol 70, no 2, pp 241-68.

Tunesi, S. (2010) *Waste management: public governance not personal guilt*, UCL Environment Institute Environmental Policy Report, London: UCL Environment Institute.

Turner, R.K., Pearce, D. and Bateman, I. (1994) *Environmental economics: an elementary introduction*, London: Harvester Wheatsheaf.

Turok, I. (1992) 'Property led urban regeneration: panacea or placebo?', *Environment and Planning A*, vol 24, pp 361-79.

Urban Studies (2001) Special issue on the neighbourhood, vol 38, no 12.

Urban Task Force (2005) *Towards a strong urban renaissance*, London: Urban Task Force, available at www.urbantaskforce.org

Verhage, R. and Needham, B. (1997) 'Negotiating about the residential environment: it is not only money that matters', *Urban Studies*, vol 34, no 12, pp 2053-68.

Walton, W. (2000) 'Windfall sites for housing: an underestimated resource', *Urban Studies*, vol 37, no 2, pp 391-409.

—

Ward, H., Norval, A., Landman, T. and Pretty, J. (2003) 'Open citizens' juries and the politics of sustainability', *Political Studies*, vol 51, pp 282-99.

Ward, S. (2004) *Planning and urban change*, London: Paul Chapman.

World Commission on Environment and Development (WCED) (1987) *Our common future*, Oxford: OUP.

Webster, C. (1998) 'Public choice, Pigouvian and Coasian planning theory', *Urban Studies*, vol 35, no 1, pp 53-75.

White, I. (2008) 'The absorbent city: urban form and flood risk management', *Urban Design and Planning*, vol 161, no DP4, pp 151-62.

Whitehead, C. (1999) 'The provision of finance for social housing: the UK experience', *Urban Studies*, vol 36, no 4, pp 657-72.

Williams, J. (2005) 'Sun, surf and sustainable housing – cohousing, the Californian experience', *International Planning Studies*, vol 10, no 2, pp 145-77.

Winter, M. (2000) 'Strong policy or weak policy? The environmental impact of the 1992 reforms to the CAP arable regime in Great Britain', *Journal of Rural Studies*, vol 16, no 1, pp 47-59.

Wykes, M. (2000) 'The burrowers: news about bodies, tunnels and green guerrillas', in S. Allan, B. Adam and C. Carter (eds) *Environmental risks and the media*, London: Routledge, pp 73-90.

Young, M. and Willmott, P. (1986) *Family and kinship in East London*, London: Penguin Books.

Zola, E. (1883, 2002) *Au bonheur des dames,* translated by R. Buss as *The ladies' delight*, London: Penguin Classics.

Zukin, S. (1989) *Loft living: culture and capital in urban change*, Chapel Hill, NC: Rutgers University Press.

Index

Page references for notes are followed by n.